"After each chapter I read, I felt the itch to keep reading. I didn't want to put Leeana's book down. More and more, I needed the message of hope to grow deeper inside of me. I've known loss and heartache. This book poured hope into my brokenness like it was water—refreshing, restorative—and I just wanted more of it. *Hope Anyway* is for the weary, shattered, and recovering. Really, it's for all of us. We all need hope. We are desperate for it and Leeana delivers it."

Anjuli Paschall, author of *Stay* and founder of The Moms We Love Club

"In her newest book, Leeana Tankersley has offered us a beautiful gift: the invitation to honor our humanity—while also knowing God is profoundly with us in the journey. *Hope Anyway* is a sacred, timely reminder for each one of us as we learn to show up fully in the world."

Aundi Kolber, licensed therapist and author of *Try Softer*

"I have a complicated relationship with hope. With tender truth-telling and profound wisdom, Leeana's words met me in my own darkness and illuminated a path for learning how to walk in the dark. *Hope Anyway* is a resilient anthem that reminds us that we don't hope because of what we receive. We hope because of Who we receive. Join me in returning to this breathtaking work again and again."

Nicole Zasowski, marriage and family therapist and author of *From Lost to Found*

"I've been waiting for this book since I heard Leeana was writing it. Sometimes things fall apart. But what happens next? What is revealed? And how can we ever be OK again? There is no guide I want more on the far side of these questions than Leeana. Her wisdom is hard-earned, her storytelling lyrical and vulnerable, and her gentleness a balm. This is a remarkable book."

Christie Purifoy, author of *Roots and Sky* and *Placemaker*

"If life finds you at the crossroads of disappointment and despair, then you know that hope feels nothing short of risky. Leeana has been there and decided to hope anyway. In her gorgeous storytelling style, she shares why she chose hope and how we too can hope anyway. If you can no longer self-help yourself up or out of the dark, *Hope Anyway* is for you. With each sentence, Leeana is setting out a bread-crumb trail through the woods—noticing the staying presence of God along the way—to lead us out into the daylight of our lives. *Hope Anyway* gives us insight into the meaning of hope and how it works to revive and expand the human soul. Leeana is one of my favorite writers; her words have served as the company of a friend as well as insightful clues for my own travels from disappointment to hope."

Trina McNeilly, author of *La La Lovely*

hope *anyway*

Also by Leeana Tankersley

Breathing Room

Brazen

Begin Again

Always We Begin Again

hope anyway

WELCOMING POSSIBILITY
in OURSELVES, GOD, *and* EACH OTHER

LEEANA TANKERSLEY

Revell

a division of Baker Publishing Group
Grand Rapids, Michigan

Published by Revell
a division of Baker Publishing Group
PO Box 6287, Grand Rapids, MI 49516-6287
www.revellbooks.com

Printed in the United States of America

Library of Congress Cataloging-in-Publication Data
Names: Tankersley, Leeana, 1975– author.
Title: Hope anyway : welcoming possibility in ourselves, God, and each other / Leeana Tankersley.
Description: Grand Rapids, Michigan : Revell, a division of Baker Publishing Group, [2021] | Includes bibliographical references.
Identifiers: LCCN 2020058631 | ISBN 9780800738525 (cloth) | ISBN 9781493430536 (ebook)
Subjects: LCSH: Hope—Religious aspects—Christianity. | Trust in God—Christianity.
Classification: LCC BV4638 .T36 2021 | DDC 234/.25—dc23
LC record available at https://lccn.loc.gov/2020058631

The author is represented by The Christopher Ferebee Agency, www.christopherferebee.com.

21 22 23 24 25 26 27   7 6 5 4 3 2 1

To Trey and Elyse

Perhaps Paul would have written for us: "Love, yes, of course, love. But for you and your time, the greatest of these is hope because now it is hope that is hardest and rarest."

—Frederick Buechner

contents

two notes for you

I WANT TO MAKE SURE you notice two things as you read.

First, the chapter titles. When we talk about hope, I think many of us—especially after the most recent months and years—are trying to figure out what and who are worthy investments of our hope.

Can we still hope in God?
Can we still hope in humanity?
Can we still hope in ourselves?

I've formatted the chapter titles to remind us there are still a number of things worthy of our hope. However, they may not be the things that we readily think of or accept. And so, in each chapter, I am proposing something that I believe is deserving of your hope anyway. After all, hoping *in* something is entirely different than hoping *for* something. These are the varying postures, practices, people, and possibilities that, when I invested even a mustard-seed equivalent of hope into them, they held. They proved strong enough to hold the nuances of my circumstances.

I offer them to you on the off chance that some days your belief in much of anything anymore is waning, and you need to see what this looks like for someone else so that you might be able to believe it for yourself.

Some of the chapter titles may seem, at first glance, in direct opposition to each other. *Wait. Am I supposed to hope in possibility or reality, letting go or holding on, my own truth or God's voice?* you might be thinking. The answer is: yes.

I believe all of these are worthy investments of our hope, sometimes even all at the same time. Discerning when and how and what and whom to hope in isn't something we are left to figure out on our own, though, thankfully. This is a good segue to the second thing I want you to see.

At the end of every chapter, you will find a short section called "Holding Hope." In this section, I have pulled out the word or phrase that is central to the chapter, and I've invited you to hold it up to the light in your own life and see what might refract back to you as a result. This is simply an opportunity for reflection, paying attention, and the practice of listening. It's entirely optional, obviously, and something you could even come back to later, but I believe engaging with these words and phrases will help blur the line between this being my story and it also becoming yours.

The longer I write and talk about faith, the more interested I am in encouraging you to develop a practice that will help you hear God's voice, your own soul voice, and the particular invitations that might be waiting for you as you get still and listen.

Set your phone timer for five minutes. (Three minutes works too. So does twenty.) Write the question from "Holding

Hope" at the top of a blank page. Take some deep breaths and listen. Listen to what you hear, jot down words and phrases and images, then spend some time responding to what you've heard.

It is completely expected that this won't always go well, produce extraordinary results, or deliver. Totally fine. My advice: Just do it anyway.

Love upon love,

Leeana

1

hope
IN THE DARKNESS
anyway

> If I say, "Surely the darkness shall cover me,
>   and the light about me be night,"
> even the darkness is not dark to you;
>   the night is bright as the day,
>   for darkness is as light with you.
>
> —Psalm 139:11–12 ESV

THREE YEARS AGO—almost exactly, as of this writing—my marriage ended. To put a finer point on it, my marriage began the extended journey of ending. As a result of this ending, my kids (Luke, Lane, and Elle) and I moved from the West Coast to the East Coast. We did the excruciating work of unentangling, and we grieved. Like just about everything in life, emerging has taken longer than expected.

15

That last sentence? I can tell you from experience, the truth of it is very hard to accept and the reality of it is very hard to endure.

But here I am, writing a book on hope. After all that. After the unthinkable happened. Why, after the lights were turned out, abruptly and without permission, am I writing on hope? At first, this book was going to be about surviving messy middles, because I was (and some days still am) in a pro-tracted messy middle. Then it was going to be about love, because I had lost a love I thought I had a firm grasp on, and all of a sudden love of any kind felt more vulnerable than I could stand. I know that messy middles and lost loves are universal experiences, so I knew talking about either of those things would be helpful.

But then, I saw something that had been there all along, though it surprised me when I saw it. It was like the wild-eyed creature that pops up even after the great cosmic whack-a-mole has done its darndest to eradicate all signs of life. You again?

It was hope. And once I saw it—a resilient and rebounding presence—I couldn't stop seeing it. Everywhere. Hope arrived somewhere along the way, and no matter how many circumstances tried to snuff it out for good, it continued.

This, I thought. *This is what we need to be talking about. Right now more than ever.*

But we need to talk about hope in a way that both reflects our realities and transcends our realities. In other words, we need to consider the kind of hope that speaks to the right-now of our circumstances but also helps us believe that our circumstances contain creative meaning. Because I believe they do.

Before we go any further, let's stop to define our terms. Almost immediately, two kinds of hope come to mind. First, there is the *help-me hope*. The help-me hope is akin to crossing your fingers and wishing something would turn out a certain way. Its prayer is a beggy *Please, please, please, please. I hope I get to go on my trip. I hope our team wins. I hope it snows.* Nothing wrong with this kind of hope, necessarily. It's just that help-me hope's success is determined by outcomes. It's all about hoping for something. The problem—in my life, at least—is that outcomes end up different from what I had planned or could control. And I can't count on a hope that comes and goes with outcomes.

The second kind of hope, which is what I've dedicated this book to, is what I might call *hard-won hope*. Hard-won hope is a product of disappointment. We don't possess it because things went well. We earn it because things did not.

Hard-won hope is not dependent on a happy ending. It's more subversive than that. Instead of hoping for a product, hard-won hope invests in the process. This kind of hope says that even if the worst-conceivable thing happens, I can remain. I can be resilient in chaos. I can be grounded in disorientation. I can even be found in loss. I can get the crap whacked out of me and still defiantly exist. This hope's prayer is always, *I believe; help me in my unbelief.*

This kind of hope makes me think of a line from Barbara Brown Taylor I have loved for years and have revisited a thousand times recently:

"New life starts in the dark."[1]

The week I received the news that my marriage would be ending, I sat in my car, confused, shocked, desperate to fix something I couldn't fix.

"What am I supposed to do?" I asked out loud.

Here is what I heard: *Leeana, you are not losing your person. You are finding your person. And your person is you.*

That's the dumbest thing I've ever heard, I wanted to yell back. *Of course I'm losing my person. Of course I'm losing everything. My house. My future. My financial security. My children's trauma-free childhood I have been desperately trying to create. What are you not getting about this? This is death.*

Deep down—and this does not mean I liked it—I knew the voice speaking to me was telling me the truest truth I had ever been told. **Losing often leads to finding, and usually we find what we could never lose in the first place and had in our possession all along.**

The last three years have been about learning to belong to myself in ways I never have in my entire life, to belong to God in ways that transcend behavior and information, and then to belong to a select few people in my life with honesty and authenticity.

Throughout it all, new life was wanting to be born. The new life of radical honesty. The new life of congruence. The new life of not abandoning myself.

Congruence would become an important through line in this story, a recurring invitation to confront those ways of being that were no longer serving me and, instead, to choose to live in a way that was consistent with who I knew myself to be. Some of us have what I call identity dysmorphia. We can't feel our own strength, hear our own voice, trust our own knowing, or see our own gifts. Congruence means we no longer live in that dysmorphia. "The person who you think you are can't handle life. But the person who you actually are, can," Elizabeth Gilbert says.[2] Congruence means we begin to live from the person we actually are. We realize our capacity for resilience has actually eclipsed our capacity for ruin.

This new life has been stunning in its arrival, but it had to go dark for a while in order to ground down, set its roots, and begin to flourish.

When we are in the darkness—whatever that is in our own particular story—the temptation is to believe, *It's over; it's always going to feel this way; I will never be anywhere else or feel anything other than I do right now.* So we try to get out too soon. We don't want to receive what the darkness is trying to give us. After all, darkness is confusing and disorienting and devilish in the way it can distort the smallest speck into a specter. We fear the darkness, and for good reason, I guess.

But what if the darkness has a purpose or, at the very least, holds a possibility? What if something is trying to be born in you? Through you?

Talk to people who are in the dark. They might tell you of small wonders, everyday miracles—like fireflies—that come to them in the form of phone calls or signs or songs. Sustaining flickers. They might also talk to you about the experience of surrendering so fully that it showed them how life was really supposed to be lived. Openhanded, openhearted. Talk to people who are emerging, and they will tell you that they wish the hard thing had never happened, but they wouldn't trade who they've become as a result.

Darkness and the time spent there expand us. I know that all we feel and see is reductive. But this is not the end of the story. Not by a long shot. In the stillness, something generative is taking root. And the new thing that is being born in you and, therefore, being born into the world, is happening entirely out of love.

Love says, "I know your deepest longings, and I will use this darkness to bring you closer to everything you really want." Love says, "I'll show up and take care of you as I promised and bring you back home. I know what I'm doing. I have it all planned out—plans to take care of you, not abandon you, plans to give you the future you hope for."[3] Love shines brightest in the darkness.

Of course you're scared. Of course you're weary. Of course you're slightly unclear about what it is you need to actually *do* in this darkness.

Incubator. Cocoon. Ground. Womb. What happens in these places? Tiny shoots, new cells, expansion, becoming, wings. What does the thing in the darkness do? Waits. Stays still. Welcomes the becoming. Pays attention. Notices invitations. Finally emerges.

In her newest novel, Sue Monk Kidd's protagonist, Ana, prays, "Bless the largeness inside me, no matter how I fear it."[4]

Here's another reason why the darkness is scary. It's disruptive. It will expand you beyond where you may want to go or thought you needed to go. It will jar status quo. It will test what you were sure you knew. This is never comfortable. Orientation. Disorientation. Reorientation. It will introduce you to the largeness inside you. And I can promise that you, on some level, fear the true largeness in you.

Try believing your life is part of a larger story, and that story is rooted in love. Try believing part of why you are here on this earth is because something wants to be born in you and through you and given away to this world. Try believing, just for the next twenty-four hours, that your greatest sense of belonging to yourself and your greatest contribution to others will come from the darkness you must lie down in.

It takes incredible courage to let something new take root in you.

The entire universe, the whole of your life, and all of the circumstances therein (but particularly the difficulties) are conspiring together to bring you home.

Home to yourself and your skin and your guts and your heart.

Home to God and his/her grace and love and invitations and presence.

Home to your neighbor and his/her challenges and beauty and needs.

It is ALL conspiring together to get you to listen, to bring you to the place you've always longed to be. But the darkness is a part of the process.

If your life feels shrouded, even from you, and you feel lost or unmoored or untethered, could it be that something new is working its way into the world through you, and it needs time? It needs time and your attention and your surrendered spirit. It needs you not to look for work-arounds but to welcome—I know this is hard—the incubation, the waiting.

What if we could join a narrative that uses every last drop of the darkness to produce new life?

If you feel like you have lost everything—everything you thought you had, everything you thought you knew, everything you thought you believed, or everything you thought you could count on—this one's for you.

If your world—external or internal—got set down sideways recently (honestly, whose didn't?), let's talk. If you lost your faith, your child, your person, your sanity, your health, your home, your security, your family, your community, your politics, your church, your business, your comfort, your sense of what was right and wrong . . . let's talk.

You are not alone or forgotten in the darkness of undoing and unknowing. You are not alone or forgotten in the hazy waiting of the messy middle. You are not alone or forgotten when it's time to emerge, expanded and exposed.

You can drop down into your wise center even when you think you can't. You can find your voice even when you believed it was gone. You can find a place to stand even when the ground you were once firmly standing on gives way.

What follows is not a pep talk to your ego. It is a reminder to your spirit. Against every last odd, I want you to remember that you can hope anyway. So, in the following pages, I have compiled all the things that helped me hold on to hope. Or, maybe more accurately, all the ways that hope held on to me.

HOLDING HOPE

God, what do you want to say to me
about "New life starts in the dark"?

2

hope
IN LETTING GO
anyway

If pain must come, may it come quickly. Because I have a life to live, and I need to live it in the best way possible.

—Paulo Coelho

WE HAD BEEN MARRIED one month shy of fourteen years when he returned from back-to-back deployments. When he walked through the sliding glass doors at customs, I knew something was off, but I wanted to believe it was simply reentry and not what I feared in my bones.

Within a couple of days, he told me we needed to talk. So we set an appointment a few evenings later to talk at the long dining room table we purchased together during one of our overseas tours to the Middle East. I knew, I think. I knew exactly what he was going to say. And also, I was sure I was wrong. There was no way this was happening to *me*, to *us*.

But when it was the appointed evening and he asked me to go get one of the most expensive bottles of wine we owned, I definitely knew the one thing I did not want to know.

Is it cowardice or courage that begins a conversation like this? Some days I still can't decide. It's strange how hard it is to decipher between two seemingly opposite motivations. Was he giving up or letting go of something that was no longer working for him?

Once the words were actually said, actually put there on the table between us, we both cried.

A few days after the conversation, we were going to a counseling appointment he had prearranged. We were to meet at the counselor's office. He was coming from work and I was coming from home. Someone watched our kids; I can't remember now who had them. It was July-hot in San Diego, and I scanned my closet looking for my own version of a power suit—something that said I wasn't done fighting.

I put on a flowy black dress with a handkerchief hem and a St. Benedict medal around my neck. St. Benedict is the father of one of my all-time favorite phrases, "Always we begin again," and I knew I needed that mantra close.

In the days between our conversation at the dining room table and the counseling appointment, I spent most of my waking hours trying to come up with the airtight argument that would somehow change his mind. If I could come up with the right reason, the right defense, the thing he hadn't yet thought of, then he would realize. He would see. This was all up to me, of course, figuring out the right thing to say to save us all.

Denial is a stage of grief.

I arrived first and sat in the waiting room until he arrived and we were both called back. We sat on the couch across from the therapist, who already knew what was happening, already knew we had talked a few nights prior.

The therapist sat close enough to us that we formed a triangle. He had a lot of compassion in his eyes. I cried from the moment I sat down. He asked me how I was doing since receiving the news, and I said, "I am devastated. It's devastating." And then I went on to review my side, my reasons why I believed this direction to be a mistake, my rebuttals.

Things had been difficult; there was no doubt. A very real part of me—one I could not admit to having—felt relief that the angst would be over. But the only thing that mattered at all was what I believed I had to save my children from.

It seemed clear to me. This was a matter of reasoning. I just needed to make the right appeal. So I did. I appealed with logic, emotion, perspective. I gave it everything I had.

But you know what? It doesn't matter. It doesn't matter if you're right or if your argument is airtight. It doesn't matter if you think you have perspective that the other party doesn't. It doesn't matter. You can't control another person. You can't convince another person. You can't coerce another person into much of anything when it gets right down to it.

About halfway through our session in the counselor's office, sitting there in our triangle, I realized something significant. *Like the last person in the room getting the punchline.* I realized we were not there to figure out how to stay married. We were there for this person to help us get divorced. It had already been decided. It was done. This was a formality, a way to make it all happen without too

25

much collateral damage. A way to make things civil, with a third party helping us.

We got the business card of a mediator and we walked to our respective cars. I sat in mine for some time. Absolutely numb. I sat until I heard the voice, an answer, a small patch of earth on which to place my next step.

Leeana, you have to let him go.

Over the following days, months, and even years, I would wrap my hands back around the situation. I would try to come up with the strategy that would have changed this for all of us. I would think and think and think. I would crawl into corners of my brain I never knew existed.

Always, when I was in my head—figuring, negotiating—I would get that same tap on my shoulder, both gentle and firm. You might know what I mean by that. And I would be reminded, for what may have been the hundredth time by then, that I was to let him go. I was to open my hands and let go. As my spiritual director has told me since, you cannot surrender while you are strategizing. It's opposing energy.

Much of life is discerning what we are to hold tightly to and what we are to set free. I still find it counterintuitive to let something go, to stop fighting by way of surrender. We think we can will something into reality, into change. Rarely, if ever, is this the case.

Sometimes we confuse hope with happy endings. If I'm a hopeful person, then I'm fighting for that happy ending no matter what.

You hear of recovering addicts who say their parents never gave up on them, never stopped trying to reach them, never quit chasing them. You also hear about parents who say the only way their child got clean and sober was because they backed up, they let go, they let the child—finally—feel the consequences of their decisions. They stopped helping. Both approaches worked, and both approaches didn't.

As with most things in life, we can't write a rule for when we need to hold on and when we need to let go. We try to do this, you know. We try to write computer programs for our lives. If this happens, then this. If we can't figure out the programming, we turn to the gurus who have or did or can. We listen to their programs, their formulas. We buy their courses.

I'm more and more convinced that faith is what happens when we actually have to go to God with our own set of circumstances, sit with God and ourselves, and experience the red-hot vulnerability of listening. This is taking personal responsibility for our lives.

After the counseling appointment, I sat outside the offices in my car on the corner of West Lewis and Randolph, and I knew that the only way out was through. I knew that the voice telling me to let him go was a familiar voice, a voice I could trust, the penlight in the cave. I decided to listen and to follow that tiny illumination.

Even when things are happening *to* us, we still have agency. We can still make the decision to take the next step, intentionally, even if it feels like all the choices are being made for us. In fact, it is important—maybe essential to our healing—that we choose. Even if the choosing is deciding to let go.

Somehow it feels safer to put our trust, our hope, in our own bargaining than to believe there are any gifts in the letting go. Lot's wife turns back to the burning city, even after she is told not to. She wants one last look at what had been, and she never recovers.

This is familiar to me, in the same way that the Israelites' bargaining, once they realize they are entirely reliant on God's provision in the desert, is familiar to me. All of a sudden slavery wasn't entirely intolerable.

Bargaining is a stage of grief too.

For months prior, I had been working on a book called *Begin Again*. I had written the entire manuscript before "the news." The voice had something more to tell me: *Leeana, you already have everything you need to walk through this*, and I knew exactly what that meant.

The etymology of the word *begin* is "to cut open" or "to open up." We cannot move into the new country with one foot in the old country. We have to open up to the new path, again and again, as clumsy and painstaking as it is.

If the new country is where you are being invited and what you are being offered, might you believe that something sacred is and will continue to accompany you as you travel? I didn't have all this sorted out entirely as I sat under the Southern California summer sun in my minivan, but I had inklings.

So, right then and there I took my hands off the steering wheel and I turned them over, palms up and open, the back of my hands against the hot metal of the Honda logo. I said, "OK," which can be the most sacred prayer we pray.

HOLDING HOPE

God, what do you want to say to
me about the prayer "OK"?

3

hope IN YOUR SELF *anyway*

We search for a missing spiritual key, but we tend to look for it outside of ourselves where it seems easier to search. But the key is inside, in the dark.

—David G. Benner

AS ALWAYS, the voice nudges me toward what I need to know, the next bread crumb. If I listen, if I follow the hint, it will lead me—kindly, with baby steps—into truth I need to be aware of. It's not that I never question what it says. But I've learned enough to know that it's some kind of answer that arrives before I ever even knew the exact question to ask.

This is one of the reasons why I still have hope in God. Someone asked me recently if my marriage ending has caused me to lose my faith.

"The opposite," I said without hesitation.

Some people go through hard things and lose their faith as a result. I get it. I really do. In my experience, though, I found God to be closer than ever, glued to my side, whispering to me as we went along. Did this save me from having to go through every single painstaking step of loss? No. But if that's what we think faith in God is—a way to bypass pain—then we missed the point of faith anyway.

Faith in God is the acceptance that death precedes new life. In Jesus we have been given a model for going into the darkness and emerging anew. We have been shown that death is part of the process of new life. And we have been given a promise that we will never be alone, even in the valley of the shadow of death. We are accompanied. We are claimed. We are carried. We are seen.

So, when I hear that still, small voice—that voice that is both within and beyond me—I can't help but believe. And when that voice said to me . . .

Leeana, you are not losing your person.

You are finding your person.

And your person is you.

. . . I chose to believe this severe mercy.

What I knew this to mean almost immediately is that a person can lose and lose and lose, but they will always have a relationship with themselves. Everything can shatter . . . and almost does sometimes. Every year you live, you learn there were so few guarantees all along.

But one thing that remains is this pesky little self. Things will be stripped away, things we thought we couldn't live without. Sometimes the stripping will show us that we were stronger than we could have imagined, and that our self— the one we assumed for so long was defective—shows up and keeps walking, keeps reaching for some kind of light, keeps looking for a way.

We will wish that someone would come along and scoop up that self of ours and save it on our behalf. We will look for a savior, or at least a fixer. What we failed to see and what we are only now learning, since things have been stripped down, is that the person we were waiting for all along was our own self.

Your person is you.

That is what the voice was telling me. Yes, you are experiencing significant shattering. It's physically painful. You can feel the breaking inside your body. Yes, all this is true. And . . . and you will have the choice to look inward, to witness yourself, to stay with yourself, to welcome yourself, to count on yourself, and to take care of yourself.

This is such sacred work that it will save you now, and it will serve you the rest of your life. Through this, you will learn the lesson that other people won't fix you, that the next relationship will not be a solution per se, and that there is something in you that is so abiding, even the most traumatic circumstances will not silence it.

So, I began to think about this heartbreaking losing as also a kind of finding (or I was at least beginning to see that it could be both at the same time). And that the finding would not involve me picking up with someone else or morphing into a new version of myself or changing any kind of external thing at all. The finding would be me coming home to me.

But learning to sit with ourselves, unanesthetized and present, is new for many of us. As Mary Karr once said in an interview, "I would rather snort cocaine and make out with the FedEx guy."[1] No kidding. No one wants to come home to themselves at first because coming home to ourselves requires us to face our longings, our habits of numbing out, our doubts about ourselves, and our decisions. Ill-advised trysts seem so much less complicated. I mean, my FedEx guy IS NOT HORRIBLE LOOKING.

Instead, I took myself to therapy. I stayed connected to my people—my family and all the Warrior Sisters in my life. I took my meds. I slept a lot. I opened a window and lit a candle and turned on "What a Beautiful Name" whenever I couldn't figure out what else to do. I made time and space to listen to the voice.

Once you know you have no control over someone else, you see that the only real choices you have involve yourself. While endlessly maddening, this seems to be an incredibly important general lesson in life because we can tend to throw good energy after bad trying to get others to figure it out—trying to get others to behave better or notice us or approve of us—and we don't have that kind of time.

Is it possible that the next bread crumb in your life is to consider what it might mean if your person is you? That all the time and attention you've been giving to fixing others or trying to get someone else to fix you is really an invitation to return to yourself?

I began trying to train my brain that every time my thoughts trailed off in the direction of the other person, every time I was spending more time on fixing things or coming up with a strategy or argument that would convince him, I was to immediately take that as an invitation to return to me. I would harness that same time, attention, and energy and ask myself how I could return it to me. Therapy. Exercise. Phoning a friend. Making a meal. Writing. Praying. What did

I need to do to take care of myself? What was the next new moment with me?

If I had focused on what I was losing, I would have disintegrated. But, by some incredible grace, the voice kept reminding me of what I was finding. *You are finding your person. And your person is you.*

"Wait a second. Hold on," you might be saying. "Is this for real? I mean, you have no idea the kind of loss I have experienced. This sunny optimism is no match for what's happening at my address."

All I can tell you is the truth as I have experienced it. And the truth is that these last three years, as I have leaned into me and the voice has led me deeper into me, I have begun to actually experience the thing I think we all want more than anything: actual belonging.

Certain questions began to emerge as I leaned into *Your person is you.*

Would you like to stop abandoning yourself?

What if the inside and the outside of your life were completely congruent?

Do you know what you want?

(Shut up, voice.)

While I basically had an official Come Apart over each of these questions, the last one is where I'll start. It's the want/ wanted dilemma. Not all of us have this issue, but those of us who do can be owned by it.

How can I be wanted? vs. What do I want?

If I order my life around being wanted, then I am not paying attention to my desires. I am paying attention to what would make me seemingly desirable. This is immediately problematic because, desirable to whom? This is a moving target. Desirable to a person, my family, my readers, the world, Instagram, the church, God, my friends? As hard as a person tries, they can never be desirable to all these people all the time.

And the attempts to be desirable, the attempts to be wanted, I have learned, are the very same attempts that take us further and further away from our center. What a bust.

The thing we thought would bring us home is the very thing that will take us out to sea. If you are looking outward, you are not looking inward. And inward, I have found, is where it has to start. It's an inside job.

So, that leads us to, What do I want?

Why is this question so simple and the answer so elusive? I began to practice this like a workout. Like eating my veggies. Like brushing my teeth.

~~Will this make me pleasing to others?~~

~~Will this increase my network of approval?~~

~~Will this help me appear special?~~

~~Will this entice someone?~~

~~Will this make everyone else feel good all the time?~~

What do I want?

This is Julia Roberts in *Runaway Bride* figuring out how she likes her eggs cooked. Remember that one? Many of you do. It matters, you know? It matters who you are deep down inside, and it matters what has been uniquely planted there in the wise center of your being. It matters what you think and what you dream about and what makes you sad. It matters how you would say it and how you would make it. It matters what you see when you look outside and what you hear when you listen to that song. It matters. Your translation of this wild and brazen world . . . matters.

Not some reflection of what you think would be worthy. No, your actual read on things. We need more of "actual."

You don't know? That's OK. You just don't know *yet*. But if you pay attention and you listen and you are more honest with yourself than you've ever been, you will begin to discern how you like your eggs.

The amount of time you spend on trying to pull something from someone else—spend at least that much time on trying to find something in you. It's all there. That's the secret. That's the million-dollar prize. It's all there already. You are not bereft or bankrupt or blind in your own soul. That is actually not possible. So, we just have to get in there, get down there, get past all the ways we're trying to keep externals smoothed out so we don't have to attend to internals.

"Bless the largeness inside me, no matter how I fear it." Remember that piece of gold?

How utterly terrifying and how strangely relieving— both—to be told that your person is you.

Now, I know that some of you have been mounting a very strategic defense in your mind as you've been reading. It sounds something like this: What about serving others? What about putting others first? What about sacrificing our own needs and wants in order to best love our neighbors?

Yes to all that. Yep.

Unfortunately, somewhere along the way, someone taught us to conflate healing, trusting ourselves, listening to ourselves, with selfishness. This is a cunning tactic because it keeps us focused on everyone else and at a very safe distance from the fire burning in our souls.

Sometimes we are so focused on others, but it is really about us. The focus on taking care of and serving others is really an attempt to feel better about ourselves. And sometimes, conversely, the time we spend getting better situated in our own skin helps us to be truly available to those we love and want to take care of for the long term. Our self-belonging actually expands our capacity to love, nourish, and nurture unselfishly.

Wow. What a mind-bender.

Let's find a way to let go of the tired argument that serving others is always unselfish and that serving ourselves is always selfish. Let's just take all that off the table. It's a ploy to try to distract us from the actual work that needs to be done, which we are likely being invited into.

I believe you have a spiritual responsibility to steward the one-and-only you. What else do you have control over? What else can you actually change? What else can you truly give away?

What do you want?

Here's what I wanted: I wanted to stop abandoning myself in order to keep other people comfortable. I wanted my life to be congruent. That's what I wanted. I wanted these things so I could be as present as possible with my kids, so I could nurture deep connections with the people in my life, and so I could give away my work generously.

If coming home to myself helps me to be more present, connected, creative, and generous, then I'M IN.

What if your person is you? What then? Just sit with it for a few minutes and see what comes up for you.

You are not losing your person.
You are finding your person.
And your person is you.

HOLDING HOPE

*God, what do you want to say to me
about "Your person is you"?*

hope
IN GRIEF
anyway

> Grief is the willingness to be claimed by a story bigger than the one you wish for.
>
> —Stephen Jenkinson

I WROTE THE FIVE STAGES of grief on a sticky note and put it on my desk, which was positioned in a central part of the house. I walked by it twenty times a day, and it became a sanity check. Sometimes, in the early stages of grief, you feel lost and like you're losing it all at once.

You want to break something and then you want to hide under your bed and then you want to make it all go away and then you want to just get on a plane to Anywhere Else But Here and then you want to go to group therapy and talk it all out. You want to paint your entire house and then sell your house and then set fire to your house—all within the same hour. So, it's helpful to have small and large affirmations of all this, things that say to you, "Yep, that sounds about right."

This exercise of normalizing a large swath of emotions, behaviors, and reactions served me during those early days of trying to cope with the implosion of my marriage and has served me at least a million times since. I heard this metaphor recently: "Emotions are tunnels. If you go all the way through them, you get to the light at the end."[1] When we're stuck in the tunnel, we're stuck in our process. The idea to put those stages of grief on a sticky note was a gracious way to keep me moving—even if it was inch by inch—through the tunnel.

I did not think up this idea. Once again, I got a clear-as-day nudge, a fully formed idea, a step to follow—all whispered to me in a quiet voice.

Put the five stages of grief on a sticky note and put it where you can see it.

Somehow, I had enough sense to listen to this divine idea. I found a pad of fluorescent-yellow sticky notes and wrote down the stages of grief. Just those five words . . .

Denial

Anger

Bargaining

Depression

Acceptance

. . . written out in a list. This is what we do, the experts tell us, when we are grieving. We act like it's not happening. We get mad. We figure out how we're going to change it. We get sad. We open our hands. Sometimes all these things happen in a span of twenty minutes. And we need someone to tell us that this is all normal, expected, even healthy. "Good job. You're doing it. Trust the process."

One hundred years before Elisabeth Kübler-Ross popular-
ized the five stages of grief, Emily Dickinson gave us a poem
about the grief process. She equates grief to the way a person
experiences the snow. Loss involves "Chill—then Stupor—then
the letting go."[2] We experience shock, then this wandering, wondering daze, and then we are able—only because of a presence
deep within us, guiding us through the tunnel—to surrender.

We need our poets and our artists and those who are paying
attention to our human experiences. They often know things
before everyone else does. They can put words to things we
can't articulate. They can find the pulse.

Sometimes things fall apart. And it's almost impossible.
And the only way things come back together again is through
this process and, finally, when we're ready and God invites,
by choosing to surrender.

Remember that surrender not only means giving up but also
means giving back. And so, every time we're able, we say to God,
"Here, I'm giving this mess back to you. I'm opening my hands.
It's an ugly tangle, a hopeless heartbreak, a disaster. I can do
absolutely nothing with any of it. I'm counting on you." And he
reminds us, often very, very gently, that he has given us what we
need to breathe and begin again. To someday even hope again.

We pray, "Let this cup pass." But for some reason, it doesn't.
It can't. It needs to stop with us. We need to drink from the
cup of suffering. It is our turn. Finally, after the chill and the
stupor, we let go. We say, "Not my will, but yours."[3] We totally
and completely let go. For right now, anyway.

Over time, we will see that we are getting more and more
current with our reality, and we are allowing the thing to fall
apart because somewhere inside we trust that it's the only
way for something new to come together.

And yet, we need holds in the darkness. Something we can wrap our hands around, something to steady us. They aren't answers or solutions, necessarily, but they are the small gestures of grace we can give ourselves when we are at our most vulnerable.

Five words.
A sticky note.

These holds can be anything, really. A eucalyptus candle that reminds you to breathe. A bouquet of bougainvillea on your table that reminds you beauty still exists. A quote from Maya Angelou on your bathroom mirror. Even a simple ritual that helps you reinhabit your own skin, like putting lavender lotion on the back of your hands.

Find what helps you hold on in that darkness, because sometimes the tunnel feels interminable. Or disorienting. Or threatening. We forget what we learned: that new life starts in the dark. And that the darkness is necessary for a time if new life is to begin.

I don't like it. I wish the seed didn't have to be shoved down deep into the ground and that it didn't have to break open in order to become what it was always meant to be. I wish we could put the seed in a pretty bowl and set it on the mantel and speak to it in Adele lyrics and it would grow. It's just not how it works.

The darkness is necessary.

These holds help us tolerate the time spent in the darkness, help us hang on in the messy middles that stretch on and on, and help us stay home with ourselves, instead of escaping. We will want to run for our lives, and we need reminders that our "lives" are right here, waiting for us in the process, the mystery, the new beginning. They are not "out there" in some perceived easier route.

Last year, David Kessler released a book about "the sixth stage of grief." Kessler was the coauthor with Kübler-Ross for their groundbreaking book *On Grief and Grieving*.[4] The five stages of grief have stood for over fifty years. But last year, after tragically losing his twenty-one-year-old son, Kessler combined his entire career of research with his devastating personal experience to suggest a sixth stage of grief: meaning.

Research shows that part of the healing of our human hearts is finding meaning in our losses. Kessler writes, "The grieving mind finds no hope after loss. But when you're ready to hope again, you'll be able to find it. Bad days don't have to be your eternal destiny. That doesn't mean your grief will get smaller over time. **It means that you must get bigger.**"[5]

The darkness enlarges us as we find meaning in the breaking open. We find new capacity to hope again.

HOLDING HOPE

God, what do you want to say to me about

Denial
Anger
Bargaining
Depression
Acceptance
and Meaning?

5

hope

IN GOD BEING GOD

anyway

Every sound I hear—He made it.

—Rumi

ONE OF THE HARDEST THINGS about hard things is that you are typically not the only one in your life who is affected by the hard thing. You likely have a network of people who are impacted, each processing their own big feelings in their own time and in their own way. What I didn't realize was how hard it would be to hold others' reactions and, consequently, resist the temptation to fix things for everyone. Maybe more specifically, how hard it would be to entrust other people and their process to God and to let God be God.

Do you see that making the decision to let go will be ongoing? We'll have a conversation with someone we love who is hurting, and we'll pick it all back up again, frantically, and then we'll be reminded that we cannot walk forward in our process if we believe we must single-handedly carry everyone else along in theirs too.

The kids and I were in Tahoe visiting family. I stood alone on the bank of the Truckee River, kids back at the house with Grammie and Grandpa. I stood there holding the entire weight of the situation as if the only way we were all, and I mean all, going to make it through was if I put everyone on my back and hiked us out.

How can I change things? How can I create a different outcome? How can I save all these people I love from having to be in pain? I had some big ideas of things I might do, things I might say, and I watched the river rush by me—racing over rocks, like it concealed an engine. Over and through the rush of all that water, I heard, *Leeana, it's not all up to you.*

I stopped. All the emails I was writing in my head. All the phone calls I was planning. All my tinkering interrupted. This intrusive message, this phrase from far away, while terrifying in one regard, was also the most freeing truth I could have been given. You mean I don't have to figure everything out, save everyone, rescue the whole situation?

It's not all up to you.

We pick up our problems and our people's problems when we lose our hope in God's potential, the divine possibilities. We forget the creative genius of the . . .

rainbow

burning bush

manna

pillar of fire

cloud by day

wilderness

mountaintop

belly of the fish

stormy sea

stable

star in the East

eccentric cousin in fur

dove

wedding

child

cross

earthquake

bread and wine

spirit

These were all God's way of saying the same thing to humanity: "I am here. I am here to help you, give you rest, give you hope. I am here to protect you, nourish you, save you. I am here. *It's not all up to you.*"

Do you need this phrase as much as I do? If we need this truth so deeply, then why do we forget it so easily, so consistently? I don't know, exactly. But it's been happening since the beginning of time. We've always needed prophets and poets, signs and wonders, to bring us back, to remind us of our history, to remind us of what brought us here, and to remind us of our place in it all.

I went to Niagara Falls for the first time last year. The surrounding strip was so garish in its tourism that I was sure the falls would be some kind of money-making letdown. But as we got closer, the water roared and the mist covered me, and everything—I mean everything—was blurred in that moment. No more wax museums. No more arcade games. No more vendors. No more neon lighting. The falls consumed anything that tried to compete.

The sound of that much water moving that quickly was so overwhelming that it scared me. The utter power. The immediacy. The absoluteness. Nothing stood a single second of a chance against it. Nothing. I was afraid of it. And I was inspired by it. Because it put me into a right relationship with nature and my life and God. Here I am. Helpless and hopeful, waiting and willing. That's what I've got.

Have you ever stood anywhere that offered you this kind of view? Somewhere that suddenly allowed you to see the whole thing in perspective, something that made you into a mystic? I think this also happened to me when I was standing on the edge of the Truckee River, trying to figure out my next steps, trying to fix things so that no one I love would have to hurt. The sheer speed and strength of the river reminded me that I was a part of a larger system, and the larger system was held together by forces greater than me.

I had to reinvest hope in this larger system, in the reality that God is God and I am not. And not only that this larger system was holding me but that it was also holding those I loved. God's arms were wide enough and strong enough for every hurting heart. In a simple prayer, just whispering a name, I could bring someone to this Help. I could say, "Please watch over him. Please watch over her. I'm out of big ideas except one: you."

During that same trip to Truckee, I took a yoga class. Our yoga instructor, Jacquline, reminded our class that most of the day we are bent forward—cooking, typing, driving, changing a diaper, reading, looking into some device, carrying a heavy load, working, working, working.

We are hunched over something or other almost all the time, so she designed an entire class for us to open up our "front body."

In other words, she was attempting to get us to completely reverse our normal posture and expose the heart. She mentioned that all the poses we were going to do might feel especially vulnerable since we were used to protecting our front body, but exposing the heart center, stretching out the muscles in our chest, would help us breathe and help us find strength in our own openness.

When I get hunchy, I think about the front body. I have found I cannot really breathe when I'm stooped and doubled over. And I certainly have no possibility for perspective. So, I think about opening up the front body, exposing her heart, stretching her chest, sending her center up, up, up to the sky.

Look up, stretch up, breathe up, open up. It's not all up to me.

Perhaps you are carrying a load you were never meant to carry, don't have to carry, could learn to set down.

You do not have to take your grief and crawl off into a corner and hold it alone. You do not have to fix all the broken things by yourself. *It's not all up to you.*

HOLDING HOPE

God, what do you want to say to me about "It's not all up to me"?

6

hope
IN REBUILDING
anyway

I hope you know it's okay if your strength looks a little different in this season.

—Morgan Harper Nichols

IT HAD BEEN ABOUT TEN MONTHS since the talk at the dining room table. Nothing was particularly contentious, but nothing was finalized yet either. Not much was clear to me during those days except a simmering longing to be closer to my family.

I flew to Virginia to visit my sister, who was going through some personal challenges, to walk into someone else's struggle so I didn't have to think about my own for a few days. While I was there, we drove through the historic part of downtown Lynchburg, on original cobblestone streets, past three-hundred-year-old brick bridges and buildings. We passed a relic of early America, a manufacturing facility that had been transformed into "Imperial Tobacco Lofts." A neon green sign hung from the roof: NOW RENTING, with a phone number below it.

Next, I did something that ended up changing everything. I allowed that simmering longing to surface. I called the number on the sign and asked about their vacancies. The property manager told me she happened to have a three-bedroom loft apartment available. She asked me if I wanted to look at it, and I decided to follow the bread crumb.

We—my sister and I—were buzzed into the building and met the property manager on the ground floor. She took us up to the second floor and opened the door to a two-story, three-bedroom, three-and-a-half-bath apartment with soaring ceilings, original wood floors, and exposed brick.

My sister later told me that it had been a long time since she had seen that kind of uncontested happiness on my face. I knew instantly that I wanted it. Absolutely instantly.

I got back to San Diego with a rental application in my bag and a desire in my heart. I asked God if this could be the next bread crumb. I had no desire to test the limits of my kids' resilience; I had no desire to be selfish or knee-jerk. But when I thought about this relocation, I tried to suspend judgment long enough to pay attention to how it felt in my body. And it felt clear.

My sister was in Virginia, my mom was moving to Virginia, and in a series of details that I never could have orchestrated, the kids and I—and soon after, their dad—were headed to Virginia.

I know what it's like not to be able to figure out how it would be possible to put any of the pieces back together again. No matter how you look at these parts, you cannot figure out how they will add up to any kind of new life. I understand. In the midst of great upheaval, we long for sweeping clarity. You know as well as I do that putting life back together again is an unfolding that typically happens one small increment at a time.

So, I just kept putting my foot into the next patch of light as it was revealed.

My kids and I arrived in July. We moved into our loft and had our three pods delivered. I ordered a couch and a twin-over-double bunk bed for the room the girls were sharing. I enrolled the kids in school and thought it absolutely other-worldly that my kids would be attending school with their cousin Jackson, my sister's youngest. The last time I lived on even the same coast as one of my siblings was in 1999.

We ate burgers from the restaurant next door to our right and we ate tacos from the restaurant next door to our left. We rode bikes down to the riverfront and ate ice cream at Maylynn's. We helped the dog adjust to urban living, even as we were all trying to adjust. Street parking. Hauling groceries up two floors. No storage. No lawn.

But we did. We adjusted. Even more, we carved out a new little life. We spent a lot of time with family, watching games, going for walks. The kids' dad made plans to relocate nearby, and we stumbled along, figuring out how to be a family. A new family. Nothing about this was glamorous or enviable, necessarily, except that we began to see that the darkness would not overcome any of us, we were all still breathing, and we were making it. Looking back, that was huge. But in the moment it felt like crawling.

In sports, we call it a rebuilding year. A team gets a new coach or graduates a huge class of seniors or starts a rookie quarterback. It's a rebuilding year, and we automatically change our expectations or lower our standards accordingly. Some years are rebuilding years, and that means things look different. We might pull off a few come-from-behind wins, but we're not expecting the Super Bowl. Not this year anyway. Showing up is its own big deal.

The year before we moved to Virginia, I was numb. But the year in the Lofts was our rebuilding year. That explains why some days felt like I was learning to move all over again. If you are too, I see you. Rebuilding. And it takes a lot more patience and courage and hope than anyone ever talks about.

Rebuilding asks us to tolerate all our longings, waiting when we're asked to wait, moving when we're invited to move. All the while navigating waves of intense, if not overwhelming at times, feelings.

When we're rebuilding, we also tend to meet up with regret somewhere along the way.

Regret means to re-weep. Terrible. One definition says it is the distress of the mind due to something done or something left undone.[1] Isn't that true? Sometimes we regret the thing we did; sometimes we regret not doing anything when we had the chance. Sometimes both, all wrapped up in the same situation.

There are two kinds of regret. One is productive, where we look back and we see specific lessons we've learned. I think this kind of regret is rare.

Most regret is a thief. It steals the present from us while we rehearse a past we can't control. Most regret robs us of our humanity. It looks back on a situation with all the information, all the perspective, and all the hindsight and judges the decisions we made when we had none of those things. Certainly, if we made a hurtful choice, we need to make amends, but often our regrets are more free-floating and gnawing. If your regret is productive, moving you forward toward wholeness and healing, then let it be. But if your regret is unproductive, taking the time you have and turning it into emotional chaos, then ask God for the grace to forgive yourself.

We can't rebuild when we're paralyzed by unproductive regret.

Additionally, we can't rebuild alone. It's not possible. So, rebuilding will also require help and support. You will need your people—the same people you've always had—who will show up for you in ways that shock and humble you even though you've known them forever. If you do not have people you can trust or if your people have been sucky, you could find yourself a community of fellow rebuilders who have gone through the exact same thing you have. A class or a support group. I cannot tell you how healing it is to be in a room with people who understand. You will also need a guide—a therapist, counselor, spiritual director—someone who can help you see where the next brick may need to go.

We also can't rebuild if we're not on our own team. If we're constantly badgering ourselves, shaming ourselves, judging our every move, we will not be able to rebuild. We'll start to stack some bricks, make some progress, and then that toxic voice inside will tell us that what we're constructing is ugly or unfit, and we will seize up in paralysis. This will likely happen no matter what, but if we can recognize it, recognize the wrecking ball that lives in our heads, we will be able to begin again.

I want you to know that it's not over for you. You can rebuild. You absolutely can. It is painstaking. It is exhausting.

But at some point—and I say this after a lot of time and tears—you will see that you aren't where you were. You aren't where you started. You will stand back, with the smallest bit of perspective, and you will see that you have participated in the moment-to-moment of a miracle.

HOLDING HOPE

God, what do you want to say
to me about rebuilding?

hope IN WHAT SAVES YOU *anyway*

> Then you hold life like a face
> between your palms, a plain face,
> no charming smile, no violet eyes,
> and you say, yes, I will take you
> I will love you, again.
>
> —Ellen Bass

LYNCHBURG, VIRGINIA, is the little town in Central Virginia where my sister, my brother, and I all went away to college. We all have lots of memories in this town, lots of history.

Downtown Lynchburg, the area where the Lofts are, is now up-and-coming but was just about no-nothing twenty-plus years ago when I was in college. Restaurants, breweries, coffee shops, and boutiques are now popping up in this historic district full of old stone and early America.

One of the things that is seared into my body from our first year in Lynchburg after my divorce is walking the dog. Every single time Rosie had to go out, she had to be taken down two floors, out huge glass double doors, and either onto the street if we were to go out the front of the building, or out to a boardwalk that ran above the James River if we were to go out the back.

Along this boardwalk were stone benches, tables and chairs, a few restaurants, some green space, and giant planters with cascading greenery, all overlooking the river. I made myself think about it as a gift every single time I went out. How else could I frame this kind of chore? I had to put some kind of spin on it.

Rosie, our black labradoodle, was (and still is) on doggie speedballs, so she was crazy every single time I left the building. It was something I had to emotionally prepare for: her pulling and barking and general desperation to get near any other living thing, but especially any other dog. She would froth and lurch and hop up on her hind legs like some sort of circus sideshow. It was so embarrassing.

Many times, we would be walking down the street and we would pass a dog going the other way. Rosie would become so frenzied that she would sort of hop sideways down the street while trying to get the attention of the other dog and still somewhat move in the direction I was now practically dragging her.

Because she was ogling and convulsing and hemorrhaging over the other dog, she would not see what was coming, and she would often turn around just as she ran straight into a pole, a meter, a stop sign. I could see exactly what was coming and I let it happen. She had to learn. It stunned her for a second. But then she'd be back at it, twisting and turning to get any kind of glimpse at that other dog.

Oh, she's such a smart breed, they all said. Really worth every penny, they all said. One of the smartest dogs out there, they all said. Fascinating. She probably ran into two dozen poles while we lived downtown. That doesn't seem very smart to me.

If she saw a dog up ahead of her, she would lift up onto her back legs only and walk that way for ten, twenty, thirty steps. I'm holding the leash, and she's walking beside me on her back legs, whimpering and retching and begging, like a seizing kangaroo. It was mortifying. She's like the Mary Katherine Gallagher of dogs.

We've been through hours of training. She even went away for puppy boot camp. But somehow this is just who she is—a dumb, darling lover. Welcome to the family.

Then there's the "picking up after the dog." Bending over. Let's pause right there. I just feel like I have evolved past any circumstance that requires me to shoot my butt up in the air and lean my head down to the point of passing out. For what? It's always related to picking up. And it's almost always related to picking up someone else's crap. Literally, in this case. But the best is yet to come. Next, I am putting a baggie on my hand, picking up something hot and mushy with only a thin layer of plastic between me and that substance, and carrying the baggie around until I can find an appropriate receptacle. I mean, I was made for more.

Rosie came to our family in a perfect set of circumstances. I found her just a couple months after we told the kids the news. I knew all our worlds were changing, and I so deeply and desperately worried about the kids. I knew joy wouldn't hurt anything. I prayed for the right dog. Seriously. I scanned Craigslist and prayed, "God, bring us the right dog. And help me to know when I find her." My criteria: a puppy, a girl, and hypoallergenic (because Luke and I both have major allergies).

"One labradoodle left in the litter," the ad said. "Ready to come home with you on December 23!" With sweaty palms, I clicked on the link. December 23 is Luke and his twin sister Lane's birthday, so I had a hunch this might be our dog. It was a girl. She was still available. She was about forty-five minutes away. We could go visit her immediately.

She was four weeks old when we met her. I took Lane with me, and we cuddled and snuggled her for a solid hour. Lane was wearing a headband with a rose on it, and the dog kept pawing at the rose. Lane said, "If we get her, Mom, I'll name her Rosie."

I was an unadulterated puddle. I knew we were getting her. God shows up in terrible messes in the most needed forms. It's uncanny.

We picked her up and brought her home on the twins' birthday. It was a tiny little fairy tale in the midst of so much heartache. We let her fall asleep on our laps at the dinner table. We let her nibble our fingers and sleep with us in our beds. We spoiled her and we received her comfort.

So, as much as I want to curse that dog sometimes, as much as I wish she were a bit more of a cool cat, I can't ever quit her. She's the crazy angel that has been constant in the midst of so much change.

After moving into the Lofts, Rosie and I walked and we walked and we walked. Past the same shops and the same restaurants and the same benches. In stifling humidity. In snowstorms. In rain. Through Fourth of July flags and pumpkins and white Christmas lights. We walked through four distinct seasons, like a movie montage, and then through a second summer and the beginning of another fall.

The walks around happy hour or dinner are what I re-member most, especially the twilight walks on the weekends. Couples on dates, having drinks together, dressed up. Girls' nights out with strapless bras and heels and chilled rosé. I spent almost all my time with kids and my mom and my sister—all of whom are fabulous company. But when I walked Rosie on Friday nights, past the patio bars, I was reminded of what seemed to be missing. I watched and tried to remember how long it had been since I had done that. If I'd ever do that again. Rosie would pull me past the conversations and the laughing and the soft lighting and the holding hands across the table. She would keep pulling me on.

Me, in a stretchy waistband, holding a bag of steaming excrement, watching the world go on without me. Or so it seemed some nights.

During our fifteen months at the Lofts, every single day I had to lie down for at least thirty minutes, sometimes much longer. And every single day it terrified me. *If I get in that bed*, I would think, *I will never get out.*

It wasn't that I felt overly depressed or ruinous. I was just tired. Soul weary. And I feared that one day I would crawl into my bed, I would set my phone timer for thirty minutes, and when it went off, I would silence it, turn over, and someone would have to come scrape me out with a giant spatula. Or maybe one of those big canvas slings on a crane they use to transport whales.

But I always got up. When it was time to go pick up the kids from school, I did it. When it was time to work, I did it.

When it was time to cook, I did it. And, as previously detailed, when it was time to walk Rosie, I did it.

What I want to tell you is that I know that feeling. The feeling of having no more resources to muster. No new magical gear to shift into. No bootstraps to pull up. It was scary to feel that level of depletion. It forced me to rely on my network, to lie down, to get through, quietly and simply. Not from a stage or in front of a crowd. But resting in an unfamiliar room or with a leash in my hand, walking through a city in total anonymity.

I walked it out. I lay down. I walked it out. I lay down. **This is how we start to put life back together again.** An unforced rhythm of grace.[1] Step by step by step. We all want to skip ahead, to fast-forward, but it takes each step in order to move from here to there.

If it's taking longer than you thought it would, than you ever dreamed possible, it's OK. You're OK. It takes what it takes. And, also, I know how eternal it all is. Absolutely eternal.

Let's talk about waiting. It's hideous. Waiting causes such a powerlessness that sometimes it is impossible to believe anything could ever change. Author Holly Whitcomb introduced me to the term *active waiting*, which is every bit as hard as it sounds, but it's also a way that we can take back some power in an otherwise passive situation. She says, "Active waiting teaches us to trust that each small step is part of a larger process—a process in which we can participate with steady determination."[2]

Walking Rosie was an unconventional and unexpected way I participated in the waiting. I'm not even sure I meant it as such, but the necessity of the chore created a sustaining rhythm.

The strangest things will get you through. It just might shock you . . . the way God ends up saving you, the way he keeps you moving. Having to take a frenzied and desperate dog out four to five times a day, having to move your feet, and even—yes, even—bend over and pick up and take care of things you'd rather not deal with. Greeting strangers on the route, sipping hot coffee or cold sparkling water, breathing real air, looking out to the James River and the exuberance of the fountain at the base of the bridge shooting water 190 feet in the air, smelling hamburgers cooking on the grill at Bootleggers and pork roasting for tacos at El Jefe, toddlers squealing on the splash pad next to Water Dog, taking in the cinnamon-sweet aroma of waffle cones at Maylynn's. The train whistle. The salmon sky at twilight.

Beginning again is so often the hardest thing we do. But these were the rhythms that helped. Rosie's rambunctiousness would match my inertia, and I would be invited to step outside yet again and walk it out. Past couples and tables and benches and trees. Past flurries and dogwoods and fireflies and falling leaves. Again and again and again. Like a labyrinth. Like a prayer walk. Like a pilgrimage. Every step an arrival.[3]

HOLDING HOPE

God, what do you want to say to
me about what is saving me?

8

hope IN MYSTERY *anyway*

Not even the world can hide you from us forever.

—Frederick Buechner

I WAS OUT for an early morning walk on Christmas Day. The dog was with me, pulling hard on the leash, my rotator cuff hanging by a thread. She lunged at every blade of grass that quivered, every bird on a faraway fence, every alluring scent. Before we had a dog, I dreamed of walking her in beautiful places and enjoying the serenity of our companionship and nature.

Have I mentioned I'm prone to fantasy?

On Christmas morning, my kids were with their dad, so my mom and I snuck off to the Biltmore Estate, a few hours away. We decided to stay for two nights as a treat to ourselves and because they were hosting a Downton Abbey exhibit we wanted to see. We had also heard the house was unparalleled at Christmastime, so off we went.

We took the dog with us because I could not secure boarding for her last-minute at the holidays. On Christmas morning, I got my coffee and took her out. The sun was bright and the sky was blue, but the air was crisp, and mist was rising up from a nearby pasture.

Rosie tugged and hopped and wound around me so that we almost tripped over each other. So, basically, it was a completely standard walk. At one point, I had to put my cup of coffee in the vertical pocket of my jacket in order to have both hands free. This was an ill-conceived solution, as you might imagine.

Betwixt and between all this mayhem was the pasture, cloaked in mist, lined with trees and a wood fence that came into and out of view depending on where the mist was moving. I could hear cows bellowing from behind the foggy curtain, but I could not see a single one. I could hear chickens off in the distance but, again, could not find them with my eyes.

We walked on and the scene changed with each moment. Every single second something shifted, lifted, intensified, dissipated.

I was sad, of course. My first Christmas without my kids. Disoriented maybe even more so. Doing what I know to do, which is to make the best of a hard situation. Create an adventure when possible. Make a memory. My mom and I even brought the deluxe Scrabble board along, the one on the turntable. This is what we do, especially when there's nothing else that can be done.

As I have gotten older, and as I have acknowledged the need, I have built more capacity to hold space for sadness while also creating goodness. The Christmas morning walk was a physical practice of this tension, a chance to walk out into my sadness and also see the cloaked beauty that is absolutely always present.

I do things like this intuitively. Yes, the dog needs to go out. Always. But it was more than that. I walked longer and farther than was necessary. I opened up a portal through which something could arrive if it wanted to. This is our work.

I stayed on the path that bordered the pasture, and I walked well past the pasture. I crunched pea gravel under my feet, and I drank coffee that had gone cold. And then, there it was.

The small voice. The familiar voice. Saying just two words: *Look again.*

I looked even though I had been already. I looked and took in what I was seeing. The dog's breath in the air. The mist hovering over the pasture, obscuring whatever it was that existed behind it. The sky. I took in the details as I noticed them, and I took in the overall scene too.

Look again.

I looked again. In the foreground, a cow was coming into focus. Something I could not see thirty seconds prior.

Look again.

I looked again. I could now see a horse, which was a complete surprise to me, as I didn't even know horses were in the pasture. I could hear the cows, but the horse was totally unannounced.

Look again.

It went on like this. Shape-shifting before my very eyes. The dog pulling and whimpering and launching up onto her back legs with each animal revealed.

Look again.

I kept looking. Again and again. I keep looking. Again and again. Looking for love. Looking for hope. Looking for humor.

Looking for nourishment. Looking for connection. Looking for beauty. Looking for the unexpected. Looking for the cow to appear after I could only hear it. Looking for the horse that was a complete surprise. Looking at how things change upon inspection, and I didn't do anything at all to create that change. I just looked. And looked again.

> The one we were looking for was there then and he is here now because he haunts the world. I think he has come to haunt us more and more until there is scarcely a place any longer where, recognized or unrecognized, his ghost has not been seen.
>
> —Frederick Buechner[1]

Did you know that the word *hope* is a word of unknown origins? I spend a lot of time in etymological dictionaries. I rarely come across words with totally unknown origins. But *hope* is one of those words.

We can't pinpoint where *hope* started, what language first articulated it. We don't know when it was formed into meaning or if it has just always been there, set in our spirit since day one. Something about this rings true. We don't necessarily drum up hope. We don't make it happen or summon it, even. It's not something we can cajole. It's more mysterious than that. It's happening around us. There, haunting us, even when we can't fully see.

Some days are hard, horrible, and just need to end. We don't have the mental health or even the desire to see. It's OK. Go to bed.

But then there are the days when we can lift our heads even a bit and look. And then look again. And things arrive. Things reveal themselves. Things appear. Even while a dog is tangled at our feet, causing cold coffee to jostle just about everywhere. Even when we're out in public in our pajamas with a coat barely camouflaging our non-bra situation.

Look again.

Put those two words in your pocket. Walk around with them close to you. When you can, look, and then look again. See how shapes shift and mist rises and clouds change and hope stirs. And you had so little to do with it all, except to allow for the portal.

HOLDING HOPE

God, what do you want to say to me about looking again?

hope
IN SURRENDER
anyway

Are you tired? Worn out? Burned out on religion?
Come to me. Get away with me and you'll recover
your life. I'll show you how to take a real rest. Walk
with me and work with me—watch how I do it. Learn
the unforced rhythms of grace. I won't lay anything
heavy or ill-fitting on you. Keep company with me
and you'll learn to live freely and lightly.

—Matthew 11:28–30

IN THE FINAL FEW DAYS OF 2019, I walked into the
woods behind my house. Our lease at the Lofts had ended,
and we were ready for the next stage of rebuilding, which
came to us in the form of a house in the woods. We'd moved
into this new house two months prior, and I wanted to get
the lay of the land. My kids were still gone for Christmas,
and I set aside a day for listening. Listening has become the

single most significant practice in my life. Listening to myself. "What do you want, Leeana?" Listening to the voice of God. "God, what do you want to say to me today?" Allowing God to be a spiritual director of sorts, asking me questions, dropping bread crumbs for me to follow.

I made coffee and poured it into my olive green Yeti so it would stay warm. I put on my coat. The trees were gray poles, and I tromped across leaves so deep, it was like walking on a mattress. I got to a spot that seemed good, and I sat down in the leaves. I took off my shoes and my socks. I don't know why I did this except that sometimes you do something almost without thinking because it seems like the exact right thing to do in the moment.

And, also, it's good to put our bare feet into nature, skin to ground. When we're trying to return to ourselves, when we're trying to get our feet back under us, shoes and socks are just impediments.

It was crisp out but not so cold that I felt uncomfortable. I had on my puffy coat and I had my hot coffee, and I—without much notice—was barefoot, putting my feet onto the spongy layers of leaves.

Then I lay all the way down. Flat on my back. I stayed for two hours. At times, tears ran into my ears.

Since the news, I have had a hard time stringing together more than a few days of orientation, focus, efficiency. I ask God for these things all the time. Clarity, a plan, energy, order.

"I need a plan. Tell me what to do," I say. "I need to know how to organize my life. I need you to tell me what to do about everything. I need to know about work and money and chore charts and how to keep the car clean and the future. I need answers to a hundred questions."

You don't need a different plan, Leeana. You need a different posture.

Stretch out.

I did.

Be still.

I was.

Turn your hands over, the voice says.

I did.

Breathe.

And there I was. Lying in a pile of dead leaves in the woods behind my new house, my feet bare, the backs of my hands resting on the prickly dried edges underneath them. Totally still. Totally vulnerable.

The voice said, *Corpse pose. I would like you to stay in corpse pose.*

I lay for some time in corpse pose. I felt breeze. I heard construction noises. I heard birds. I smelled earth and leaves. I saw a rapidly changing sky overhead.

They say corpse pose—*Shavasana*—is the most difficult of all yoga poses because it requires us to be aware, present, and totally surrendered. We are not stretching, straining, trying to hold a particularly spectacular position. We are not showing off our yoga clothes or even able to look around at what everyone else is or is not doing in relation to what we can or should be doing. We are not up in our head, engaging the ego. We are simply awake, quiet, still. Control relinquished. Allowing things to unfold. Making ourselves available to becoming.

We ask for a plan. We receive a posture. This is infuriating and also resonant. A posture requires trust. I have so often wanted to stand at a safe distance from my own life and figure everything out. I want to stand back and think, consider, analyze. And move in only once I have things figured out. The problem is that often the only way to figure anything out is by stepping into it. Learn through experience, trial and error, sometimes even learning the hard way. Sometimes, and this is the most counterintuitive thing in the world, walking to the center of our lives, toward the things we want and believe we need the most, and lying down. Palms up.

But this is much harder than it looks, isn't it? Just lying there. I mean, what good could that possibly do? I was asking God to deliver order in the midst of all my chaos, or—maybe more accurately—I was asking God to show me what to do so that I could secure order for myself. "Which bins from Target?" "Which capsule-wardrobe plan?" "Which subscribe-and-save products?" "Show me what to get so I can create order."

("So I can create order.")

There is nothing wrong with being organized and strategized. Whatsoever. In fact, the right routines keep life running smoother and more efficiently. But the right routines can become our way of controlling things. And, of course, the things I wanted control over were never going to come from The Container Store.

There in corpse pose, God gave me a small gift. God brought to mind the creation story, the original order-from-chaos narrative.

First this: God created the Heavens and Earth—all you see, all you don't see. Earth was a soup of nothingness, a bottomless emptiness, an inky blackness. God's Spirit brooded like a bird above the watery abyss.[1]

It was going to become something from nothing. It was going to become earth and water and sky. The chaos was going to get ordered into something new. But before it became anything at all, before it was called forth, before it emerged, it was just still, and the Spirit was hovering. God's voice would soon be heard, but there was a cosmic beat before a word was spoken. The mystery of the Spirit spread out over the stillness.

New life starting in the dark.

The Spirit maternally spreads her wings over us as we wait, there in our most vulnerable posture. We wait for the new creation to be called forth. We wait to see what we will become. We wait to hear the voice. We wait for the next rebuilding stone to be handed to us. And while we wait, we are not alone. The Spirit holds a kind of vigil there as we experience our human vulnerability.

Is it possible that this mystery is expansive enough to hold all of our hope? The mystery of the Spirit commingled with our surrender in the darkness and God's voice. Let there be light.

The darkness is never so dark that it cannot hold new life.

I lay there in the leaves. My heart was weary. So very weary. I was scared because I didn't think I could produce anymore. I didn't think I could create anymore. I didn't have the stamina. *I'd rather get in bed. I'd rather read a romance novel. I'd rather snuggle with my kids and never change out of my pajamas.* And on the days when I did have the energy, I was confused about what I should do next, which direction I should pursue, what endeavors should get my attention.

I stayed there in the leaves as still as I could stand to be. Palms up.

Open your eyes.
Look.
Look again.

I saw the sky through the fingery branches.

Close your eyes.
Open your eyes.
Look.
Look again.

I saw that what had been blue just seconds before was now completely gray, clouded, shrouded.

What did you do?
I did nothing.
I lay here.
The entire landscape changed, and I lay here.
What did you do, Leeana?
Nothing.
What did you do, Leeana?
I noticed.
You noticed.
That's what I'm asking you to do with your life. To pay attention. To notice. To translate what you notice. That's it.

Corpse pose requires courage. Not only because it's a posture of vulnerability but also because it is a posture of non-striving. It takes courage to stop whipping up our own efforts or pushing and trust that something just might come out of our engaged surrender. Actually believe that our striving will not be what ultimately delivers success.

Corpse pose is the embodiment of faith, trusting instead of treadmilling. **Creation did not have to create itself.** As Archbishop Desmond Tutu says, "God created order out of disorder, cosmos out of chaos, and God can do so always, can do so now."[2] This is the hope. Something is at work that is beyond, before, beside, and beneath us. Can do so always. Can do so now.

This is why self-help will never be enough. We need a Higher Power. We need God. Each and every one of us. We need to come to the end of ourselves, through some circumstance in life—the end of our capacity, creativity, brilliance, research, personality, good looks—and realize that the answer is both within us and beyond us. It rises up because of the Spirit hovering and God speaking. Hope in our hustle is not enough.

Lie down in the middle of your life. Lie down in the leaves. Dig your heels down past the cushiony bed of what has fallen. Dig your heels into damp dirt. Find a shoot of green. If there isn't one, look up. Look past the branches that skulk through the sky. Look into the sky itself. What is there?

What do you see? Is it blue? Close your eyes for thirty seconds and look again. What do you see? Is it now clouded, covered and uncovered?

What is actually happening? Not what you think about what's happening. Not how you can change what is happening. But what is happening? Here. Around you. In this sacred stretch of space.

And as you are there, still and present, picture the Spirit with outstretched wings, protecting every vulnerable place in your being as you wait for the voice of God to call forth new life.

HOLDING HOPE

God, what do you want to say
to me about surrender?

I've listed a few additional "Surrendering
Practices" in the back of this book.

hope IN DISAPPOINTMENT *anyway*

> Maybe we are called upon to say not yes, because yes is too much for us, but to say maybe, maybe, because maybe is the most that hope can ever say.
>
> —Frederick Buechner

AFTER JESUS is crucified and resurrected, he meets up with two disciples on the road to Emmaus, though they do not know it is him. He asks them, "What are you discussing so intently as you walk along?"

They tell Jesus that he must be the only person in all of Jerusalem who hasn't heard what is going on. So they fill him in, telling about "the things that happened to Jesus, the man from Nazareth." They say, "He was a prophet who did powerful miracles, and he was a mighty teacher in the eyes of God and all the people. But our leading priests and other religious leaders handed him over to be condemned to death, and they crucified him. We had hoped he was the Messiah who had come to rescue Israel."[1]

"We had hoped . . ."

We had hoped he was the answer to our problems. We had hoped he was the promised rescuer. We had hoped he was who we thought he was. But it turns out he wasn't, after all.

I've been there. Haven't you? We had hoped the virus wouldn't rob us of graduations and weddings and travel and time with loved ones, not to mention all the human lives. We had hoped that we were far past where we actually are in terms of anti-racism in our country. We had hoped that someone would rise up out of the election soup who would galvanize our entire country as one. We had hoped that, because we try to be good most of the time, bad things wouldn't happen to us. We had hoped cancer wouldn't come for one of ours. We had hoped our marriages would survive. We had hoped at least one of our children would be a slightly better athlete. We had hoped aging wouldn't knock on our door quite so soon. We had hoped . . .

We had hoped we could get pregnant. We had hoped for more money, the right job, or, at the very least, a substantial side hustle. We had hoped for sober parents, reliable vehicles, a less hysterical pet. We had hoped for slimmer calves, more interesting friends, a smaller appetite. We had hoped we could outgrow the trap of becoming our indignant and defensive thirteen-year-old selves every single time we go home for the holidays. We had hoped leaders could be trusted and that life didn't feel so terribly short. We had hoped . . .

We had hoped he was coming to rescue us. But, as you can see, that didn't happen. The two men trudge along with the world's biggest hope hangover. Of course we can all relate.

Underneath the gratitude we all feel for the things that remain in our lives, there is always a layer of unrequited hope. We had hoped. We wished it had been different. If we were in charge, we would have made sure it was different. We nurse the hope hangover too.

But, as with the disciples on the road to Emmaus, something is happening that we cannot see. And, like them, instead of acknowledging the possibility that things are happening in and around us that we cannot perceive completely, we believe it's all over.

Like them, we too trudge along, commiserating, and what we don't realize—what we literally cannot see or recognize—is that the thing we had hoped for is *right there. What the disciples didn't know is that what they had hoped for, they had also received, they were actually witnessing.* They just didn't realize it yet. Jesus was the answer to their problem, but the answer arrived in a series of events that was unrecognizable to them because they believed it would all look (and feel) significantly different.

Has this ever happened to you? Over time you see that what you wanted, what you actually longed for deep down, had in fact arrived. But it did not resemble the packaging you had been looking out for.

We see this theme threaded throughout Scripture, which means it's an important clue into our humanity: we expect problems to be solved by the solutions we can come up with. But we're working with God, here, who works with a totally different set of possibilities.

You had longed for deep connection and creative work and intimacy. And when you actually looked at your life, you saw that you had it but maybe not in the ways or through the mediums you had been looking out for or had expected.

In his gorgeous essay *The Hungering Dark*, Frederick Buechner writes about hope. He taught me that there's a Hebrew word for hope—*gawah*—that means to twist. He says that we take "a hundred little strands of hope that we twist together to make a cable of hope strong enough to pull ourselves along through our lives with. But we hope so much only what is reasonable to hope for out of the various human possibilities before us."[2]

Buechner says we take tiny threads of hope and twist them together so that we can be sure we have something to hold on to. We basically hope for good things to happen and for bad things not to happen. He calls this hoping in the possible. He says this kind of hope is sturdy enough to get us out of bed and through the day, but it is still human hope. And we have access to a divine hope that is a kind of fantastic madness because it is not hope in the possible but in the impossible.

The hope in the impossible is the hope we must harness when we are lying in the dark, believing that new life is forming but is also not yet. The disciples missed this. All they saw was the darkness. They could not see Jesus. Literally. They had put hope in their own vision of the way they believed things would unfold, and when it didn't happen, hope moved into the past tense. *We had hoped.*

But, divine hope reminds us that something mysterious and generative is at work in the darkness. The Spirit hovers. And the Spirit was hovering on the road to Emmaus, I believe.

The Spirit was saying, *Look beyond what you can see. Look past your own perception. What you had hoped for all along has actually already arrived. Look. Look again.*

If it is true that new life starts in the dark, and I believe it is true, then hope is what reminds us, there in the inky blackness, that something new and alive is on its way. Even though it is imperceptible to us right now. The very fact that it is imperceptible to us should be a clue that we are on the right track. It means we are not twisting together our own strands of hope, but we are, instead, waiting on a divine hope that is always already lying beside us and hovering over us there in the darkness.

Hope is not born in us because we have somehow escaped disappointment in life. Hope is born in us only because we have experienced deep disappointment. Hope arrives only after we have been through the unthinkable and we see that we did not evaporate, we did not disappear. We were not abandoned after all. We somehow continued.

So, so many—too many—have lost their faith entirely. They have continued to look at despair and disappointment as proof that what they had once hoped in is now certainly, and with certainty, unresponsive.

My question is this: Is it possible that new life, in all its nuances and forms, may simply not be recognizable yet? But that does not mean it isn't right there, walking with you even now.

Maybe. Just maybe.

We want to pick up our own remnants of what's reasonable and fashion solutions out of the prettier parts. We want to invest in what we believe has potential.

Divine hope says,

It is all sacred
Bless the waves, the wilderness, the cliff's edge
Bless the valleys, the rivers, the endless and the ended
paths
Bless the storms, the birdsongs, the single tear
Bless the hunger, the thirst, the desert
Bless the heart, the ear, the eye that sees
Bless the rain, the scattered and the shattered seed, the
incandescent moon
Bless the light and bless the night
It is all sacred

Amen.

HOLDING HOPE

*God, what do you want to say to
me about "I had hoped . . ."?*

hope
IN SMALL WONDERS
anyway

You can cut all the flowers but you cannot keep
Spring from coming.

—Pablo Neruda

THE FIRST SUNDAY I walked into my church, we had just
moved to Virginia. The church was five minutes from Imperial Tobacco Lofts, and some friends encouraged me to check
it out. I put my kids in Sunday school, and I sat by myself on
an old wooden pew. Surrounded by total strangers.

"Blessed are those who mourn," the pastor began, "for they
shall be comforted." He spoke with such great empathy from
this particular line in the Beatitudes. I cried the entire ser-
mon. How did I find my way there on that Sunday? How had
I been led to that pew on the day he would be talking about
those who were grieving, those going through loss, and the

promise of comfort for those who need it most? How does that happen?

These small wonders are sustaining, aren't they? When we are disoriented, they help us believe that we might actually be on the right track.

The leaves on the trees around my house mute the vibrancy of the sunrise so that the colors dissipate and scatter most months of the year. But for a few months, once the leaves are completely gone, my living room will turn rosy pink for about ten minutes each morning, and if you go to the back of the house and look out toward the woods, you will see that the sky is on fire. It melts away as quickly as it arrives, but for those few minutes I forgive—thank, even—the hundreds of spindly gray sticks in my backyard for letting go of their leaves.

The only time you can see this miracle is when everything that used to be in my view is gone, everything is laid bare. Loss takes, but it also gives. You get eyes you didn't have before.

When you realize that nothing is guaranteed, you start to look for the promises. These small wonders were there all the time, but we get focused on the big picture and we miss the very things that would nourish us the most.

The pandemic began to escalate in March. Within days, even hours, everything shut down. Events, offices, sports, churches, schools, parties, retreats, meetings, transportation, appointments, gatherings, restaurants, travel. Everything was a no.

I sat at my desk in my bedroom, where I work. I like working here because I've put my desk in front of the largest windows, so I can keep an eye on the trees. The emails rolled in. No. No. No. No. But the trees had other ideas. There, on every single branch, tiny green buds were emerging. Each day things grew grimmer in the news. And each day the buds multiplied and magnified.

It was defiant in the way that hope can be. I would shake my head, smirk, as I saw spring arriving against all odds. The world was dying. But even a global pandemic could not stop the trees. The tiniest buds symbolized resurrection. And this is what we have to be looking out for.

My big kids finished elementary school while everything was shut down, so no school graduation ceremony. We had to mark the milestone anyway, so we did it ourselves, in my living room. My sister put on her doctoral regalia, the cap and gown that was once our dad's, and led the procession while my niece piped "Pomp and Circumstance" through her iPhone. My brother gave the commencement address, an adaptation of the story of Nehemiah. My sister conferred degrees, homemade diplomas. My mom gave the closing prayer, along with a lagniappe ("lan yap")—a Creole word from her Louisiana roots meaning "a little something extra"—for each child. Goody bags with silly string, potato chips, and five-dollar bills were torn into.

In certain seasons, our prayer is the prayer that every human throughout history has prayed in some form or another: "How long, O Lord?"[1] How long will it feel like this, look like this, taste like this, smell like this, sound like *this*? How long?

I wonder if God's answer to this is not that there will be a destination we reach where all the hard is alleviated. Not here and not now, at least. Instead, we are to look into what is there already, waiting to be seen. Look for the lagniappe, the little something extra. Look for the small wonders. This is the diligent work of the seeker.

This is an invitation to inventory the small wonders in your day, to notice the smallest detail that lands in your body with lightness and ease. Anything that brings you out of your head and into your heart. The small wonders leak in through our senses, so what are your senses saying in any given moment?

Could anything grow at your house? Herbs in the windowsill? Pumpkins in a raised bed? Tomatoes in a tower garden? Fiddle figs by the front door? Boxwoods by the driveway? If something could grow, could you help it along? Help it find a place in your rhythm, help nourish it and tend it? Just seeing basil grow will change you.

How long has it been since you've been touched in a meaningful way? In a way that didn't demand anything of you? Paying someone to rub your feet or knead your shoulders is not out of the question here. Research shows we need nonreciprocal touch in our lives. We need to be touched in a way that asks nothing of us in return. Touch that is simply for our own nurturing.

What makes you laugh? Not polite, society laugh. Guttural. *Saturday Night Live* reruns? *The Office*? Whoopie cushions? Retelling old family stories, like the time your mom sent your brother to the garage after he spilled Coke on the new carpet? Jen Hatmaker Facebook posts? Whatever it is, lap it up when possible. "Joy is not made to be a crumb," Mary Oliver tells us, and I think this is especially true in times of sorrow.[2] We need the physicality of laughter.

Is there a fragrance that calms you? Lavender or citrus? Peppermint or cedar? Eucalyptus or vanilla? It's OK to burn the good candle or diffuse the special oils. It's OK to allow yourself to breathe good things. I have rosemary by my front door, and when the air turns humid, I can smell its woody but-teriness anytime the air stirs. A soothing aroma can change the current of your day. Even opening a window can create possibility.

Are there any babies in your life? I have a baby nephew who was born to our family seven years after the last grand-child. We got a ninth inning homer, and we are all drunk with love for him. He slaloms through us, wobbly, while we cheer and video and hand him Cheerios. In the midst of some of the very hardest years for our family, we got a baby! A thick-thighed, blue-eyed, curly-haired little guy, and the whole thing just tickles us all. There are so few things in life that can't be momentarily soothed by rocking a snuggly, mushy baby.

Does something taste especially good going down the hatch? The hottest coffee you can stand—so dark it's almost thick? Coffee so cold and so light it's one shade darker than milk? Ice water with lemon? English Breakfast with honey? Make sure you take a split second to experience it, not just consume it.

Almost every night when I am falling asleep, I say this breath prayer in my head: *God I rest* (on the inhale). *In your peace* (on the exhale). Slow. Deliberate. Mindful. All the churn-ing from the day goes into those two simple phrases.

We can convince ourselves that in a world this big, this fast, the winners are the ones who can move even faster. But I'm not convinced this is actually what any of us want. Don't neglect the sun hitting a sleeping child's face. The way it highlights the freckle below her bottom lip and shows off the length of her lashes. Watch how the sun rises and sets every day without any breach in its rhythm. Watch how dogs love their people and waves break and leaves turn and skies shift. Whatever you do, don't neglect the small wonders, as they hold the possibilities we must welcome, a way we hold on to hope anyway.

HOLDING HOPE

God, what do you want to say to me about the small wonders in my life?

12

hope
IN REALITY
anyway

Hope, unlike optimism, is rooted in unalloyed reality.

—Dr. Jerome Groopman

WE ALL HAVE HOPE in the way we think life should be, the way we likely believe it *will* be. But what happens when what we had hoped for, what we had assumed, what we planned on, is not the reality we are presented with?

My nephew, Jackson, is one year, almost to the day, older than my twins. He spends a good deal of time at my house, hanging out with my son, Luke, and he is full of spitfire and sass. He does spot-on Southern accents, calls Luke "City Boy" and me "Boomer," and likes to ring my doorbell and pretend to be selling me something I already own. A ball from the yard. One of Rosie's old bones. Something he dug out of the garage.

I open the door, and this is the conversation that always commences:

"Oh, hello," I say, as if we've never met.

"You might not want to invite me in since I'm a stranger," he says.

"You're right. I don't let strangers in my home. What's your name?" I ask.

"Sales," he says without hesitation.

"And what is your last name, Sales?" I ask.

"Man."

And then he proceeds to extort me.

Jackson is a hammy adolescent with personality for days, but he didn't start out that way.

Jackson was diagnosed with autism when he was seven, and he did not do a whole lot of talking prior to then. In fact, he was nonverbal for many years. He was frustrated too. It was difficult to know how to help him when he was agitated and unhappy.

But over time, he has found humor and friendship and YouTube. Of course, he can sometimes be just plain obstinate. Immovable.

After we moved here to Virginia, I made it my mission to help get Jackson into Sunday school. We would all go to church together. My kids would peel off to Sunday school, but Jackson would sit in the main service week after week. Sunday school was a "hard pass," he told me. I decided to push on the subject with him while we were standing in the foyer of the sanctuary, people chatting and milling all around us.

"Hey, J."

"Yeah?"

"Why don't you go to Sunday school with Luke? It'll be more fun than sitting in the service."

"I'm not getting sucked into that black hole," he said in a voice that was unmodulated, just to make sure I could hear him over the crowd.

"OK, great. No problem," I said back to him. And that was that.

I related the story to my sister, who was in the bathroom when the conversation took place, and she reminded me of a Christmas Eve service when Jackson yelled out, "Baby Jesus is a bad guy," because he was mad he had to go to church.

So, at least we were making some progress. Jackson was willing to sit in church. Sometimes he would wear his headphones and play on his Switch, but sometimes—if a certain pastor was speaking—he'd mute his game and play it without headphones because he liked the sound of that pastor's voice, which is a bit Kermit-the-Frog-y.

My sister would make trades with him. He had to stay in church for twenty minutes, and then they could go out and sit in the café. My sister would stretch this "twenty minutes" as she was able to, but once Jackson found out that there was a huge digital timer on the top of the balcony, he was harder to trick.

"That's it. Times up," he would say. Again, still working on the voice modulation.

That same year we all traveled to Florida together to celebrate Christmas with my brother's family. My sister and her two kids and my three kids and I got in her minivan and drove to Greensboro, North Carolina, so we could take sixteen-dollar plane rides on Spirit Air. I told my kids they could each pack a backpack and that was it.

We also decided that it would be festive to wear ugly Christmas sweaters since we were traveling on Christmas Day. My sister bought mine, which looked more like a sexy elf than anything.

The seven of us arrived in Greensboro, parked the minivan in long-term parking, hitched up our backpacks, and walked into the airport like something out of a movie. We started toward our gate, and it became clear that Greensboro was very into our attire. We were getting lots of love from the people, and that's when Jackson started what could only be described as yelling, "Merry Crisis, everyone. Merry Crisis."

We made it to Fort Lauderdale though. And once we got there, it was obvious that what seemed like a great idea in Greensboro made us look like the Clampetts in Fort Lauderdale. We might as well have been hauling Styrofoam coolers with duct tape through the terminal.

That same Christmas, Jackson became a "cat dad." The pound had free-cat day, so my sister, Laura, jumped on it. They found a petite little gal named Amy Farrah Fowler, which Jackson immediately turned into incredible variations like "Ready, Ame, Fire."

He wrapped that cat up like a burrito in Big Blue, his blanket, to the point that it was unclear if she could breathe or not, and he would play his Switch while she purred from somewhere inside the fabric. Amy and Jackson became best buds.

Every Thursday night, Jackson spends the night at my mom's house. They are like an old married couple. Jackson will hold my mom's purse when needed, help her read the manual for her new car, take out her trash, and go get her mail from her mailbox. They sit on matching recliners and eat pizza and watch *America's Funniest Home Videos*, *The Price Is Right*, *Wheel of Fortune*, and *Jeopardy!* He will do anything for Gran.

There isn't a week that goes by that our extended family doesn't celebrate how far Jackson has come. He has transformed into a charming, clever comedian, who—despite some very real challenges—is thriving.

What I've learned from Jackson's life is that sometimes our hope is forced to morph from what we thought we wanted into new visions, new possibilities, new outcomes. Seeing this new hope—one firmly rooted in an unalloyed reality—fulfilled is one of the most extraordinary gifts.

We no longer take baby steps for granted. We no longer make any assumptions. We no longer forget gratitude.

I am writing this book in 2020, a year that has been incomprehensible on so many levels. A global pandemic. A race reckoning. School and work schedules obliterated. Businesses unable to survive. A highly charged election. Our nervous systems have revved and sputtered, our anger has elevated, our camps have become more polarized, and we have seen different sides of people we love. Perhaps good, resilient, helping sides. But, perhaps, bigoted, small, disappointing sides too. As we all know, each one of us is capable of good and bad behavior.

I have watched my people and many more throughout this country rise, speak, pivot, and search for the light, even when the light was a skinny shaft trickling through a pinprick of an opening. So many people just kept looking for the light. And when they found it, they didn't hoard it. They wrote about it and shared it and celebrated it and invited others to stand in it too. It all felt generous in a way we hadn't been before.

Our realities shifted significantly and almost overnight, and so our entitlements changed too. We no longer expected much of anything to be the way it was. We had to become conversant in flexibility and adaptability and lowering of expectations. Somehow, though, when the good things happened—however tiny—we held on to them a bit longer, shined a light on them a bit sooner, said our thanks a little louder. And it was good.

Has anything at all gone totally differently than you'd planned? Than you'd hoped? Is it possible that this new reality could still be fertile ground for expectation, even if that expectation must be adjusted? And in your new expectation, could hope still flourish? Maybe not grandiose. Maybe just a grain. But a grain can be great if we are willing to celebrate it, willing to see the possibility in it.

Oncologist, hematologist, and hope researcher Dr. Jerome Groopman says, "Belief and expectation—the key elements of hope—can block pain by releasing the brain's endorphins and enkephalins, mimicking the effects of morphine."[1] Hope is that significant, that powerful, like a drug to our brains. Especially, he says, when applied to the actual events of life. Not the way we wish things had been. The here-and-now, real-time events. He calls this clear-eyed, true hope.[2]

When we were living in the Lofts, Jackson, my sister, and I all got stuck in the elevator because my daughter Elle had dropped a lid to some of her makeup in the door track and jammed the door. Another resident heard us in there, trapped, and like the Jaws of Life, he was able to pry the door back just enough to stick his arm in to us. His hand came through like somebody reaching up from the grave. We gasped. Then cheered. Saved.

We thought for sure this meant that Jackson would never get in another elevator again, but what we failed to remember is that what is even more traumatizing to Jackson than being trapped in an elevator is any form of exercise whatsoever.

When he realized that he would have to take the stairs if he were to boycott the elevator, he jumped into the next elevator happily and immediately. We all laughed about this together. A shared memory. A funny story. An analysis of a situation. A proactive choice. Fluidity.

At one time, we did not have these things. They weren't possible. We celebrated what we had then, what worked then, what was possible, even as we hoped for more. We celebrate what we have now, what has become possible. And we have celebrated every small step in between.

HOLDING HOPE

God, what do you want to say to me about maintaining hope in my current reality?

IN LOSS

> Only Hope was left within her unbreakable house.
>
> —Hesiod

LAST YEAR my beloved friend Ken Hamilton died. I've spent untold hours with Ken and his wife, my dear friend Elaine. We've all celebrated together, dreamed together, traveled together, worked together, eaten together.

Ken was an avid runner, intellectually brilliant, and wildly successful in business. He was about to become a grandfather for the first time (to twins!) when he developed gallbladder cancer, and then he was gone. In an absolute blink: gone. He died three days after the twins were born. When he was diagnosed in late November, he had been the picture of health. He died in early April.

He and his family engaged in every form of cancer intervention—Western, Eastern, traditional, naturopathic, spiritual, dietary, relational. I don't know many people who had more to live for than Ken did. A thriving business, an amazing family, a growing nest egg, two babies, a gorgeous property on Orcas Island, a community of friends and family who loved him.

My life intersected with Ken's life in some distinct ways. I was a friend, a neighbor, an employee, and a loved one, and like probably everyone who knew him, I feel as though I had a unique relationship with Ken.

In other words, I got to see Ken in a variety of contexts. And I got to see him up close in those various contexts. I watched him take risks in his business. I watched him plan trips with his kids. I watched him hold my babies. I even watched him argue with his wife a time or two. And I watched him tirelessly give legs to her extraordinary vision: to provide a therapy practice housed in an old renovated home in the heart of San Diego.

Ken was always taking care of us. Always spoiling us, even—as was Ken's way. We were the recipients of his generosity a thousand times over.

One Sunday morning, Ken picked up my kids and took them to Pacific Beach for breakfast. He said he wanted to give me some time to myself, and the excursion reminded him of time he used to spend with his kids. While they walked the boardwalk, my daughter Lane stopped to watch an oil painter who was capturing the ocean and selling his various paintings. Ken bought one of the paintings for her—wild waves crashing on the shore.

When I told my kids of Ken's passing—and may I emphasize that he was family to them—Lane went and got the painting and we sat on the floor in a circle, crying together, while Lane held the painting Mr. Ken had bought her on her lap. Hugging its edges like a teddy bear.

"Think of all the things he did for us, Mom," my youngest, Elle, said. "He cooked us the best chicken. Who is gonna make us chicken?"

When my kids' dad was deployed, Ken and Elaine would come over at bedtime and Ken would always spend extra time with Luke, man-to-man. He'd get in Luke's bunk bed and they'd talk about mortgages and interest rates and how it was that a person could figure out how to sell things on Amazon.

I told my kids I was flying to Mr. Ken's memorial service, and Lane said to me, "He sure was an exciting man, wasn't he, Mom?"

One of my favorite contemporary poets, Mary Oliver, has a poem with a famous question at the end. She writes:

> Tell me, what is it you plan to do
> with your one wild and precious life?[1]

Ken taught us all a little bit about what it looked like to live a prayer, a prayer of gratitude, what it looked like to completely exhaust this one wild and precious life.

In March, just a few weeks before Ken passed, I flew to San Diego to visit Ken and Elaine. I felt a nudge to go, and when I walked in their house, I knew why. Ken had declined significantly.

The last night of my trip, Ken told me to go to the bar and get the bottle of wine he had left out. It was a bottle of Faust that I had given him for his birthday the year before. Ken is hard to buy for and very resourceful. He really wanted this bottle of wine but wasn't able to find it right off, and I had made it my mission to find it and give it to him for his birthday. I think it surprised him that I was able to find it, which really delighted me.

He asked me to open it. And I insisted he have a sip with me even though I knew it didn't taste good to him anymore. He no longer had a taste for it, but he sipped it with me anyway.

I think he knew he was dying. Maybe before the rest of us were ready to believe or accept it. And even in his decline, he was choosing how to take care of us. Let's toast. Let's make another memory together. While we still can.

Tell me, what is it you plan to do with your one wild and precious life?

I said good night to him that night. I had to get up early to catch a flight the next morning. We hugged and he kissed me on my cheek, and I kissed him on his scruffy, scraggly cheek that was so thin. I told him I loved him. And he told me he loved me.

And as I walked down the hall to their guest room, somewhere inside I knew I would not see him again.

I'm grateful to Ken for always finding ways—both subtle and completely over-the-top—to take care of all of us. From New York to Orcas to Napa to right there in his own backyard.

I'm grateful for his holding my babies and smoking meat and opening good wine. For experiences and trips and creating spaces where we could all be together. For listening and advising and helping me through the most difficult years. For showing up.

I'm grateful for the ways he taught us about beauty and about enjoyment, how to not feel guilty for really living. He understood abundance.

One of the last pieces of advice Ken gave me was a metaphor about interval training for long races. I was in a very difficult season and he told me about a training secret. Run hard when you can and then rest. That's how you have the stamina to go a long way.

Ken ran hard. He raced and played and worked and loved and adventured and toasted and invested and led and explored.

And now, may he rest.

The Hamiltons' backyard was filled with folding chairs the warm April day of his memorial service. Filled with grief, shock, and one tribute after another too.

What if Ken would have lived? What if the interventions would have miraculously worked? What if all the prayers and all the reasons why it made sense for Ken to live would have come through? What if Ken would have beaten every odd?

But he didn't. He was taken from us too early, too abruptly, too finally.

Anne Lamott writes that "'Why?' is rarely a useful question in the hope business."[2] We all know this to be true, and we all still ask the question. Why? Why are some healed and some not? Why do some live and flourish and some wither? Why do some marriages make it and some don't? Why? And who chooses? Who is in control of all this seeming arbitrariness?

I have read theologians, concentration camp survivors, oncologists, psychologists, poets, and I have read Jesus Christ himself, and I still cannot write a single sentence that would satisfy my own questions of why.

The only thing I can come up with is this: Since we cannot entirely decipher why hard things happen to some and good things happen to others, we have a choice to make. Will we still consider hope to be a worthy investment anyway? Or will we abandon hope?

Researchers will tell you that the opposite of hope is not actually despair; it is apathy. "I just don't have the energy to care anymore."

Despair still cares.
Apathy is empty.

If you look up the origins of the word *apathy*, you will find some interesting roots: "without suffering"; "*a + pathos*."[3] No pathos = no sadness, no despair, no anguish, no sorrow, no misery.

In other words, the opposite of hope is numbness. What I know about numbness is that you can't cherry-pick what parts of you stay numb and what parts of you stay alive. If you numb hope, you also numb love, joy, pleasure, desire, excitement, and fulfillment.

Sometimes numb is all we've got, and that's OK, for a time. But numb is not alive, not a way of living. I get it though, believe me. *Hope* often feels synonymous with *trick*. Frederick Buechner writes, "To hope for more than the possible is to court despair. To hope for more than the possible is to risk becoming the ones who wait. . . . To hope for more than the possible is a kind of madness."[4]

Is it pure madness to hope in hope? Yes, on paper, it is pure madness to put any faith at all in the impossible. But—and this is what I keep coming back to—I do not believe there are gifts in the alternative. I will not live my one wild and precious life in service to numbness, cynicism, or spiritual apathy. I will not.

And so, I must develop an orthodoxy that transcends outcomes. If my faith hinges on good things happening, then perhaps it isn't faith at all. Maybe it is something akin to wishing. It's not that outcomes are irrelevant. Of course they matter. In many ways, our days on earth are marked by these outcomes. But is it possible for our lives to be defined by something more?

We know hope can heal, hope can buoy, hope can change things, hope can lighten a load; but we also know that hope doesn't always keep the darkness from descending. Some say, "Hope isn't a strategy." I get that sentiment, and I also disagree. For me, there are a lot worse things than putting my hope in hope. I don't think it's blind and I don't think it's misguided.

Do you know the story of Pandora's box (which was actually a jar)? In the Greek myth, Pandora—who is said to be the first human woman—is given a jar with all the world's evils inside. Her name literally means "one who bears all gifts," as she herself had been endowed with gifts from each of the gods.

She is told to never open this jar but, of course, she does. Immediately, all the contents of the jar escape, and evils are released into the world. Everything in the jar escapes except one thing. Hope remains.

Only Hope was left within her unbreakable house, she remained under the lip of the jar, and did not fly away. Before [she could], Pandora replaced the lid of the jar.

—Hesiod[5]

Many different theories exist on why it is that hope was the only thing that didn't make it out. These differing theories echo my own wrestling.

Some literary theorists say that hope is the most precious of all things, and so the gods made sure it was kept back to be protected. Some say it was withheld from man as a punishment, that we would never actually be able to possess hope entirely. Some go so far as to say that hope is the greatest of all evils because it causes humanity to live with false expectations, and so it was the mercy of the gods to not let it loose on us.

I've turned this story over and over, and what I come back to is simple: hope remains. And something about it is so powerful that it couldn't be lost. Of all that was lost, hope is the one thing that remained. Something about it was *that* significant. So, whether this was by means of punishment or protection, maybe it doesn't matter so much. What the story tells us is that hope stands alone in its strength and consequence.

Maybe the myth is trying to tell us that not even death is a match for hope.

HOLDING HOPE

God, what do you want to say to me
about hope in the face of loss?

14

hope
IN HOLDING ON
anyway

But the soft cord
with its little frayed ends
connected us
in the dark.

—Naomi Shihab Nye

FOR THE LAST FIFTEEN YEARS, I have been in a group with some exceptional women. When we started out together, we met weekly, and we intentionally opened up our lives to each other. We told our life stories, we shared what was really going on in our hearts and in our minds, and we learned how to listen. Our group has morphed over time, but all these years later, we're still holding on to each other.

During a particularly desolate stretch of quarantine, we were collectively lamenting the vacuum of inspiration and creativity and even just the resourceful energy required to get things done. I had offered a line from Anne Lamott that I return to often, a comment about writer's block. She says, "Sometimes you're not blocked; you're empty."[1]

There was a communal nod.

This group is full of firepower. Ten women spread out across the world these days. California, Montana, Colorado, Washington, Virginia, Oman. At one point, we all lived in San Diego, but we have been scattered across the globe now, due to life and callings and loss and love. Something binds us all together though, something steady and immutable. I like to call it WhatsApp.

We have walked side by side through death, divorce, miscarriage, marital disharmony, job change, illness, birth, infertility, a pulmonary embolism, addiction, cancer scares, and now, a global pandemic. You look at each of those things in a list and they seem like just words. But if you've ever gone through even one of the things on this list, then you know that each one of these things is an entire world, an entire life, especially to the one experiencing it.

We have sent plants and Amazon robes and scented candles and lip gloss. We have held hands and walked beaches and poured drinks and cooked dinner together. We have sent handwritten notes and gift cards and prayers. We have celebrated books and babies and businesses. We have snuck away together. We have disagreed and cried together too.

To provide a little inspiration, Erica got on our group chat and read us the poem "Supple Cord" by Naomi Shihab Nye. Erica recognized that we were all, perhaps, empty in our own ways, and she took it upon herself to read this selection to us, a poem about two siblings who each held the end of a long cord, stretched across their shared bedroom, as they lay in bed each night waiting to fall asleep.

She read us this piece as a way to sink beauty in under our skin, and we all teared up as we listened, each on our own, whenever we had a chance to log into the app. If absolutely nothing else, just to be reminded that someone is holding the other end of the cord—imperfectly, likely, but there nonetheless—was a grace.

> A person standing alone can be attacked and defeated, but two can stand back-to-back and conquer. Three are even better, for a triple-braided cord is not easily broken.[2]

I read somewhere that hope is desire combined with expectation. A desire is something we want, but we cannot control the outcome. This is different from a goal, which is something we want and can control the outcome of. (I learned this from my spiritual director.) What happens when we want an outcome but we have no control? What happens when things are just not arriving in the way or the timing that we need? What happens?

The only thing I know to do in these situations is to hold on. Specifically, to hold on to the people in our lives who will hold the burden of hope for us. Sometimes remaining hopeful is too heavy. We are too far into the cave, too surrounded by darkness. We have no perspective and we have no resources.

I have spent a lot of time over the last three years turning to the people who have made it their business to hold hope for me, to hold the other end of the cord, to say, "I'm here and I will not let go."

Most every day that first year after the news, my sister would call me. We lived on opposite sides of the country that year, but she would time the call for when I was getting in the pickup line at school so we could chat. Just checking in, she would say. And then she would listen. Ten short minutes while I waited in line for kids. "Checking in . . ."

My sister-in-law, Elyse (aka Mumsy), would send me texts that always held hope for the future. She would tell me she was believing in new life, even if I couldn't see it yet. This mattered.

At least a couple of times a week my brother would call too. He'd make me laugh, advise me, tell me I'm awesome. He'd say, "Keep kickin' butt," or something like that, every time we'd get off the phone.

I think last Easter was an all-time high when it came to cord-holding. My extended family gathered at a cabin in the woods for some much-needed regrouping. I was in transition, my sister was in transition, and my mom was in transition. And this was not necessarily bringing out the best in us. We were mopey and paralyzed; perhaps some of us were even slightly victim-y. But I won't name any names.

We gathered at a cabin we Vrbo'd for Easter weekend and were met with no less than sixty-seven pieces of taxidermy, all of which we were instructed COULD NOT BE TOUCHED. Signs, placards, threats were everywhere. We had eight children who were basically not allowed to touch anything indoors. Yes, there is a giant stuffed bobcat on the coffee table, but don't even think about it. Yes, a huge turkey is sitting on the floor right when you walk in the front door, but do not even look at it. Try having an Easter egg hunt in these circumstances.

We didn't realize this when we arrived, but my brother, Trey, had prepared a speech, and the first night we were there, he sat us down and gave us a talking-to, a real down-by-twenty-at-the-half talking-to. And I'm telling you right now, IT WORKED.

Sometimes we hold the cord with the utmost tenderness, and sometimes we use our end of the cord to whack some sense into the other person. The latter was Trey's approach. One might call it tough love. Here's the gist:

"Our family is awesome," Trey says, his voice raised. "Mom, you're awesome. Laura, you're awesome. Leeana, you're awesome. But nobody's on brand right now. You guys need to get yourselves together. Other people think our family is awesome. Other people even want to *be* in our family because of how awesome it is. We are leaders. We are butt-kickers. And we need to start acting like it. NOW! We do not need to settle for mediocre. We do not need to play small. We do not need to be anything other than who we are, which is awesome. I love you. Now GET BACK ON BRAND. GET BACK OUT THERE, AND GET IN THE GAME."

Nobody blinked for, like, twenty-five minutes. By the end we were all crying. He was totally right. We had lost our way because of so many hard things that were happening in our family. Trey reminded us of the family brand, and it's simply this: We. Are. Awesome.

I have gone back to Trey's #ONBRAND speech one hundred times. I'm wringing my hands. Or I'm on the sidelines. I'm letting other people dictate my decisions, my boundaries. I feel lost. And then I think to myself, you know what Trey would be doing right now? He'd be shaking his head and looking at me and saying, "You're awesome, and this is not on brand." AND HE'D BE RIGHT.

We lost our security deposit at that house, but I think it may have been worth it. A recommitment to our family brand all while a white-tailed deer, a rainbow trout, and a guinea fowl looked on.

That season in our family history was dark, but just the knowledge that someone who cared was on the other end of that rope, waving it wildly, even, was salvation.

You need people like that. It doesn't have to be your biological siblings, but what a gracious gift if it is. It could be a band of wild women or a brotherhood. Anyone who is willing to hold the other end of the rope for you.

"I'm holding hope for you. I'm believing on your behalf."

When you lie down at night, that cord of concern firmly in your hand, do you know someone you can ask to hold on to the other end? They can be in the same room, household, family. But they don't have to be. They could be on the other side of the globe, and it will still work if the something that holds you together is mutual.

Don't allow yourself to lie down in the darkness for too long alone. Send a message on WhatsApp. Record a Marco Polo. Let a safe word fly through your text messages. My sister and I simply send "cabin" if things are really bad, and the other knows to bring a forty-two-ounce iced tea ASAP.

When I moved to Virginia, my college roommate, Ashley, was living here with her family. She informed me that we would be working out together three times a week at her gym. I told her I was out of shape and tired and not sure if I had the time or the money. She looked at me, her smile never changing, and said, "OK. I'll see you on Monday."

And three times a week I dragged myself into the gym and took my seat next to her on a rower to warm up. Some mornings I would cry while we rowed our five hundred meters. Some mornings we'd just laugh. Some mornings we would bemoan our soreness or talk about each other's leggings. It was medicinal.

Ashley held the cord. Steady. Consistent. Solid. With uncompromising strength. And it mattered. It mattered greatly.

If hope feels too heavy to hold, it's OK. It happens. But don't go too long without letting someone who loves you know that you need help holding on. And if you know someone, a sister or brother—biological or chosen—who is bearing a huge burden, send this:

"I am holding hope for you. I am believing on your behalf."

Maybe holding the cord looks calm and tender. Maybe holding the cord is a simple text or call saying, "Checking in . . ." Maybe it looks more like snapping the cord real hard to get someone's attention on the other end and to remind them of who they really are. Maybe it looks like not taking no for an answer. Maybe it looks like a weighted blanket Amazon-Primed to the front door. Maybe it looks like all of this at different times.

With all the letting go there is to do in life, sometimes it feels really, really good to have someone who will hold on.

HOLDING HOPE

God, what do you want to say to me
about who is holding hope for me?

15

hope
IN YOUR TRUTH
anyway

The soul speaks its truth only under quiet, inviting, and trustworthy conditions.

—Parker Palmer

I WAS ONCE IN A CAR with someone who went absolutely blind with road rage. It was so startling and so violent and so terrifying that I almost opened the car door and tried to get out while the car was moving.

After some time and much more screaming and swerving and swearing, the episode evaporated. I sat down to dinner with the person and could barely breathe. The person chirped, "Do you want an appetizer?" as if the last twenty minutes never happened. I sat, trying to decide if I should ask to be taken home, if I should get up and call an Uber, or if I should just turn the page, switch gears, and enjoy the new moment.

I could barely talk, and my hands were shaking. I said, "I'm going to need a minute to recover from what just happened back there on the road."

The person looked up from their menu, perplexed.

"That had nothing to do with you," the person said to me. "It was between me and that a-hole."

There I was. Stuck. Let me tell you how much I like being stuck. ZERO likes.

Do I "ruin" the evening by speaking up? Do I honor my own experience with honesty about what just happened and how it was affecting me? Do I override myself and my emotions and my body so that we can just "have a nice evening"?

In a complete vacuum, the answer to this situation is obvious. You choose yourself. You honor your experience. You protect your truth.

But, as many of us know, especially if you have ever doubted your own interpretation of events as perhaps invalid, speaking up for yourself, trusting your own data-collecting and conclusions, and risking frustration and anger from the other party . . . these can be such debilitating forces that we just end up shutting down and joining the party with whatever gusto we can muster.[1]

I don't want to ruin the evening. I shouldn't ruin the evening.

NEWSFLASH: THE EVENING HAD ALREADY BEEN RUINED (AND IT WASN'T BECAUSE OF ANYTHING I DID OR WAS GOING TO DO).

I don't want to make the other person upset.

I would rather take on the burden of being upset so that the other person does not have to face the consequences of their actions and choices.

It is my responsibility to keep peace at all costs.

The cost to keep this peace will be me, every time.

I can tell you many stories of abandoning myself. This is one that comes to mind immediately. My own reality of terrifying events was completely disregarded as false, and I was left with a choice to either stick beside myself and my own trauma or smile and order some sauvignon blanc.

I chose to smile and order a drink, and I've had to forgive myself for that. It wasn't good for me, and it wasn't good for the other person. Sometimes we think keeping the peace will support the other person, but it doesn't. My brother once said to me, "Sometimes the most loving thing you can do is create boundaries." So, so true and so, so hard.

I will choose myself. I will protect myself. I will honor myself.

There will be consequences every single time. Disappointment. Anger. Backlash. Punishment. Others will send all this our way subtly or overtly. It will likely be held against us. This is further proof that we do not belong in close range to these people. We are not safe. But could we, at the very least, learn how to be safe with ourselves?

You do not need to spend any more time trying to get unavailable people to see you and love you, I heard the voice say to me recently. *We are spending exactly no more time trying to convince anyone. We are no longer doing that. It's abusive to our own soul.*

When we realize we are learning the practice of staying with ourselves, listening to our own experiences and perceptions as valid, we will feel relief. A very sensitive part of us can now begin to trust the rest of us. Do you know how fragmenting it is to have parts of you that don't trust other parts of you because you override and abandon them when they try to raise the red flag?

Could we at least stop knowingly and willfully abandoning the most fragile parts of ourselves? Abandon = desert, leave, forsake, vacate, walk out on, leave behind. Yowza. Those are hard words to hear. Maybe someone abandoned you, and you learned from their behavior and believed the message that you were a vacant storefront, left to crumble, a bad investment. Maybe you don't even know you're doing it—letting the lie lead. Maybe you don't realize until you're locked in a car with a crazed driver and you cannot find any of the words you need.

The hope is that the severity of the situation will finally get our attention, and we'll realize the slow simmer that has been our self-abandonment. We will finally see it—boiling over—because there's no other way to interpret the events. This is not to say that we need to come down hard on ourselves or punish ourselves for not knowing sooner or doing it all better. This is simply a threshold that will present itself, and once we know, we can't unknow.

The hope is that a new kind of self-care will gradually be possible, one in which we take care of, instead of ignore or condemn, the jittery, skittery self that lives in our skin too.

When we begin to pay attention to the part of ourselves that is plugged in to what's really going on, we will begin to be a person who is—wait for it—congruent, self-possessed, clear on what we will and will not tolerate. And some part of the mayhem will be worth it. Because it helped you find your way back to you. It helped you trust you again, or maybe for the first time.

"Put Jesus in the car with you, Leeana," my spiritual director says. She wants me to close my eyes and go back to the moment of freeze when I couldn't protect myself. "What would

Jesus say if he were sitting in the back seat, witnessing this entire incident?" she asks. I wait for some time, until I can feel the discomfort and the fear and the anger rising up in me. I wait until my eyes are stinging and my fists are clenched. I wait until my heart rate is up and my anxiety is tangible. And then I hear it . . .

"You're allowed to choose yourself, Leeana," Jesus says to me from the back seat. "You're allowed to choose yourself."

Is there a person or a situation in your life that is asking you to vacate your own values over and over again? Do you churn in the presence of this person, at the thought of this situation? What will it cost you to believe your own experience?

Close your eyes and put Jesus in the car or in the room or in the office or on the phone with you. Have him right there, witnessing. I'm not saying he will tell you exactly what he told me. But I do know that he will point you toward love in that moment. He will help you remember all the things we forget when we're just trying to keep the peace.

Likely, he will give you permission to put some hope in the part of yourself that knows, deep down, the truth. Because the truth has so much more potential than a lie.

HOLDING HOPE

God, what do you want to say to me
about honoring my own truth?

16

hope IN POSSIBILITY *anyway*

Let a new life happen to you.

—Nayyirah Waheed

I CHOSE THE WORD *CONGRUENCE* as my word last year. To be congruent means "to come together." I decided that coming together is what I really want for myself. The inside and the outside of me coming together. The head and the heart coming together. The bruised parts and the shiny parts coming together—equally important, equally loved.

A synonym for *congruence* is *resemblance*. I like the idea of making choices, aligning my life, choosing my priorities in a way that resembles me. Is my life a resemblance of me? Or is it a resemblance of what someone else told me it should be?

I decided on this word because of what I call "scaffolding." Scaffolding is the structure around your life. When you go through loss or transition, some of the scaffolding of your life is removed. Your "knowns" are no longer there.

For example, when I lived in San Diego, I was invited to speak regularly because it was a big city with lots of groups and gatherings, and so there were always opportunities and invitations. When I arrived in Virginia, I was in a small town and basically anonymous, so the speaking scaffolding that had been a part of my life was now gone.

When your marriage is over, a very significant scaffolding falls away. Where there were once another person's opinions, preferences, and desires, there is now nothing.

When you move, social scaffolding—time spent with neighbors, outings with friends, certain weekly rhythms—disappears.

When the scaffolding is removed from your life—either by choice or by necessity or by accident or by force—*the things that were creating structure and direction are also removed.*

This is very disorienting at first. What was once a known is now a void, and it's unclear what to do with that void, if anything. It's scary because you begin to see these things that provided clarity, context, rhythm, and substance for your life are now gone. Some choices had been made for you, in fact, and now you are on your own to make those choices.

After the disorientation, there is a realization. What you have now is something quite significant: you have space. You have space in your life, and you get to decide what you will do with that space. This is terrifying/euphoric. The space is not super comfortable because it's new and it's . . . well . . . empty. But it's there, and you can feel it. And something in you sees it for what it is. An opportunity.

What will you do with this space? For me the questions included, Now that you can load the dishwasher however you want, how will you load it? Now that you can wear whatever you want without a single comment from someone else, what will you wear? Now that you can put whatever duvet cover you want on your bed, what will you choose? Now that you are not speaking every week, what do you want to do with your voice? Now that you don't have standing social commitments, what do you want to do with that time?

Some of these examples seem inconsequential, I'm sure. But they actually are not. They are the small clues that help a person meet up with themselves again. What do you want? How do you want to do it? What do you want to choose? Where do you want that to go? You begin asking yourself how you would like this, how you would do that, where you would like to go. What starts as small forays into self-knowledge becomes consequential inroads into self-possession. The space is scary at first. I won't lie. You begin to see where you abandoned your own preferences and desires. You see where you compromised in healthy ways and where you gave up in unhealthy ones.

I would ask myself, *If it's true that my person is me, then what do I want?*

One of the things I wanted to do was cut off my hair. I had been wanting to do it for years, actually. Since the news. But I wasn't ready, until I was ready. Do you know what I mean? In January I chose congruence. And so in February I asked a perfect stranger to cut more than ten inches off my hair. And she did.

I cried. A good cry. "All that hair was holding so much grief," a friend said, which was so true. Truer than true. I let go of what someone else may want for my hair in favor of what I wanted. I didn't even care if I liked it or not. I just wanted to do it as a symbol.

Right after the haircut, I wrote a note to myself, "I am crossing over. Leaving so much behind. Ready for what's ahead. Today was an act of self-possession, an act of moving forward, a celebration."

When you start to realize that so many of the "governing voices" are gone, you start a new relationship with your own soul voice. You start to get a bit clearer on what you want, what you need, what's important to you, what matters to you. It's very subtle and quiet at first. It's very uncomfortable at first, too, because what if what you want is now actually possible? And what if that carries with it a lot of vulnerability?

I'm thinking of a story about Harper Lee, the enigmatic author of *To Kill a Mockingbird*. Did you know she had patrons who supported her for the year she wrote *Mockingbird*?

She was a writer. Everyone around her knew it. She knew it. But she could not focus. She could not sprawl out. She worked full-time for an airline in order to support herself, and this did not give her the time and space she needed to let her voice off the leash. Until one Christmas when her friends gave her a check for $1,000 and told her to take a leave of absence from her job and write. To see what happened.

What happened is that she wrote a history-making, history-changing book in that year. A Pulitzer Prize winner, to be exact. A seminal work on race and justice that is read avidly to this day.

The other side of this story is the fifty-five years after the wild success of *Mockingbird*. Lee now had all the money in the world and all the time in the world and she was never able to produce much of anything again. She wrote an American classic at age thirty-four, and she died at age eighty-nine, and we have practically nothing from her in those fifty-five years. People in her life tried. They tried to create structure and deadlines and incentives for her, but it never worked.

What a mystery.

The risk of space is that we find out. We find out what we've been wondering all along. And maybe we don't want to find out. Maybe the illusion is far more appealing than the reality.

If only I had some space, I could become . . .
If only I had some space, I could say . . .
If only I had some space, I could go . . .
If only I had some space, I could write . . .
If only I had some space, I could love . . .

So, when the space comes, it can also come with pressure. It's exciting to have tons of freedom, and it's scary to have tons of freedom. Sometimes it's easier and clearer to have the guardrails determined for us, and it's harder to have to do the work of discerning our own desires and preferences. It's scary to open ourselves up to the vulnerability of hope and desire. It's scary to open ourselves up to regret. It's scary to welcome possibility.

Ask yourself a few illuminating questions:

What do I never regret?
What do I sometimes regret?
What do I always regret?

Somehow regret really gets to the heart of what matters most to you and what doesn't work for you, what's serving you and what isn't. If you're wanting to fill some of the space in your life with congruence, answer those three questions for yourself. You might be surprised what comes up for you.

Sometimes things fall apart. And it happens because underneath it all—all the loss, all the pain, all the confusion, all the wandering—something true and strong needs to be revealed. Maybe it's something that's always been there. Maybe it's something newly formed. Either way, sometimes things fall apart so they can come back together in a whole new way. A way that is, finally and graciously, congruent.

I have this quote in my kitchen, sent to me from one of my Warrior Sisters, Linsey. Elizabeth Gilbert says:

> I'm choosing happiness over suffering. . . . I'm making space for the unknown future to fill up my life with yet-to-come surprises.[1]

The hope is that somehow in the newly formed pockets of space in our lives, we might leave a bit of margin for some surprising gifts. We might leave some room for possibility.

HOLDING HOPE

God, what do you want to say to me
about welcoming possibility?

hope
IN VULNERABILITY
anyway

And yet I decide, every day, to set aside what I can
do best and attempt what I do very clumsily—open
myself to the frustrations and failures of loving, dar-
ing to believe that failing in love is better than suc-
ceeding in pride.

—Eugene Peterson

HAVE YOU GONE THROUGH SOMETHING that
makes you feel disqualified? Or at the very least separate?
Different? Segregated? Isolated? Is there some kind of letter
on the front of your shirt? Do you belong to a club you'd rather
not claim?

Bankruptcy Club
Divorced Club
Widowed Club

Lost a Child Club
Infertility Club
Unemployment Club
Addiction Club
Wayward Child Club

I remember driving to a speaking engagement after I had made the news public. A very small whisper inside me knew I had hard-won hope to share with the audience. I had something important to tell them, something I knew they'd be able to come back to when their worlds were crumbling. But there was a much louder voice than that whisper. It was doing its best to convince me that I was disqualified. I was no longer a reliable source of much of anything because of this failure in my life.

Graciously, the small whisper kept going:

Is it possible that there are other people in that room who are hurting too?

Is it possible that there are other people in that room who are wounded too?

Is it possible that there are other people in that room who feel disqualified too?

Is it possible that there are other people in that room who would be deeply comforted by hearing your story?

After Jesus was killed, he appeared to his disciples in a private room. They were mourning his death, disoriented and lost. They had just walked with him, listened to him, watched him heal and restore. They knew he was someone special. They knew he was bringing in a new way of doing things, seeing things, talking about things.

But then he was gone.

And if they were anything like me, they would have been saying something like, "How did I not see that coming? It was all too good to be true."

Without warning, he appears in a room where they are all gathered, days after his death.

> "Why are you frightened?" he asked. "Why are your hearts filled with doubt? Look at my hands. Look at my feet. You can see that it's really me. Touch me and make sure that I am not a ghost, because ghosts don't have bodies, as you see that I do." As he spoke, he showed them his hands and his feet.[1]

And to prove that it is really him, Jesus stretches out his hands and shows them his scars from the crucifixion. He raises his tunic and shows his side where he had been cut open when the soldiers confirmed his death.

There is poetry in this. Jesus, Son of God, Son of Man, proves who he is by showing his wounds. He authenticates himself by showing his scars.

We show people our slick exteriors, and they are not sure. We show people our enviable strength, and they are not sure. We turn over our hands, we show them our side, we expose our stories, and they say, "I believe you."

The beautiful poet David Whyte talks about our vulnerability, which comes from the Latin word *vulneras*, meaning "wound." This is the place where the world has access to us. The true, real us. He says we each have our "own doorway of vulnerability **which you must walk through**."[2]

This is because our greatest wound is actually a portal, a doorway, to our greatest healing. It has the potential to bring us home to ourselves, if we'll walk through. Our instincts tell us to head for greener pastures and smoother seas, to reject any kind of dis-ease as unnecessary. But having gone through an unimaginable loss, I can tell you just about everything I wanted to reject had a gift for me.

This got me thinking about all of us.

What if the things we want to ignore, skip over, abandon, shut down . . . are the very things we are to learn to welcome? We learn to welcome what reduces us. We learn to welcome what pulls at the seams of everything we thought we had sewn up. Despite the vulnerability these roads produce, we learn to love them anyway.

Whyte echoes this idea. He says there are three illusions we are all protecting in our lives, and—in his estimation—the entirety of humanity is helping us protect them.

The three illusions are these:

1. We can construct a life that will keep us from vulnerability.
2. We can construct a life that will keep us from heartbreak.
3. We can construct a plan that will allow us to see the entire path.[3]

He says the reality is that none of these are true or possible. But we live as if they are and as if they should be—perhaps that we are even owed these things.

What we often fail to see is that in our attempts to create a life that is impervious, invulnerable, we are not actually living in reality. What's more, our porousness, our vulnerability, is our greatest gift to the world.

You can go to conferences and listen to people with microphones tell you that if you just strategize hard enough, you will be able to figure "it" all out. You can purchase their products and follow their programs. It's all helpful. But only to a point. Only to the point that your life collapses—or theirs does.

Then what?

You thought all along that it would be your mastery that would take you into new places in life. But it's not. Turns out, it's your vulnerability.

The greatest challenge of the last three years for me has been to tolerate the obsessive urge to be somewhere other than where my life is right now. Some days I could not stand how hard it was to be here now, to be where my feet are, to not have things more stabilized, to allow life to lack so much clarity, to hold deep longings, and to wait without any promises. To remain pliable and willowy and movable has been almost impossible at times.

I know what it feels like to want to jump straight from the shock to the all-better and not have to pass through any of the actual vulnerability.

What helped, you might be wondering? I'll tell you. It helped to know that even Jesus Christ himself was wounded, and his wounds are what he revealed to his people.

Look, here are my hands. Here is my side. This is my hope. Wounds are not the end. They are, actually, the seeds of a new beginning.

HOLDING HOPE

*God, what do you want to say to me
about welcoming my wounds?*

hope IN HEALING THE WORLD *anyway*

He charges us to proclaim the message that heals
and restores our broken relationships with God and
each other.

—2 Corinthians 5:19 The Voice

LADY GAGA TOLD OPRAH in an interview,

When I talk to God, I say:
Tell me, whisper to me
In whatever language
I will decode you
Whisper to me
How I can help heal the world
And I will do it
Even if it hurts[1]

Most of us want this, I think. Maybe we can't articulate it so beautifully, but we want this. We want to help heal the world, join the Spirit's work in the world, with whatever resources we were given on the day we were created. We see that people around us are hurting, polarized, contentious. We want to be a part of the solution instead of the problem. But how?

How can you and I help heal the world? I always believe our poets, artists, and saints are the ones who have a sense of this first. So I'm going to turn to four of them, in addition to Lady Gaga, to lead us here: Mother Teresa, Pádraig Ó Tuama, Jericho Brown, and Saint Augustine.

Let's start small. If it's true what Mother Teresa told us (and I think it is), "If you want to change the world, go home and love your family," then one of the most significant ways we can help heal the world is by loving our people. I understand—even as I write this—that we can't change our people, we can't fix them, we can't solve their issues, or get them to behave a better way. But that's not love anyway.

Loving our people is about investing in the people closest to us, praying for them, listening to them, not being too busy for them . . . these are acts of healing too. Perhaps our first and foremost. So, if you don't know where to start, start with your partner, a quiet child, a hurting teen, a new mother, an aging parent. Right there in your circle. Right there in your neighborhood. Right there in your home.

Starting small, in your own living room, is sometimes the hardest place to extend healing love. Often it's easier to mount a mission to the other side of the world and serve strangers than it is to choose a soft answer, a listening ear, or a compassionate posture for those with whom we have entrenched dynamics. I wonder if that's why Mother Teresa thought it was such a revolutionary act. It forces us to navigate some of the most difficult patterns in our lives. Having to love close-up changes us, and I'm sure Mother Teresa knew this was the first step to collective change: individual change.

Next, I believe we can heal the world through empathy. I really do.

In 2017, a very important thing happened. A movement that started eleven years prior went viral. It was called the "Me Too" movement, and it was a way that women, predominantly, could raise their hands and say that they too had been victimized by institutional misogyny, rape culture, sexual assault, boys-will-be-boys locker-room talk, and gross handsy men. Thousands and thousands and thousands of women said, "Me too. I was victimized in the church, in corporate America, at my university, in doctors' offices, by people who knew better and while others turned their heads. Yep. Me too."

We relearned through the Me Too movement something we had known from molestation and rape research. The assault is traumatizing to the victim, obviously. But what can be even more traumatizing, create more lasting and irreparable damage and compound the trauma, is when others refuse to believe the victim when she has the courage to speak up and speak out.

How many little girls came to their parents and told them that a nasty uncle was being inappropriate with them and the parents defended the uncle, told the little girl she must be misinterpreting his actions, told her it was her problem, or that the uncle was "family" and an "elder," so they needed to respect him? How many little girls carried the weight of not only a terrible secret but also blame, dismissal, and distrust from the very people who were supposed to be protecting them?

What we must take away from this is that when someone has the courage to begin speaking out against a system that has marginalized and victimized and traumatized them, the very worst thing we can do is tell them that it's their fault and that they got it wrong, again.

I have been deeply burdened by this as we have watched racism and racial tension escalate in our country. We had people coming forward en masse and saying, "This has been horrible for me. I'm terrified, I cannot walk down the street peacefully, I am constantly looking over my shoulder. I am tired of having to explain privilege to the people who benefit from it every day."

And then thousands and thousands and thousands of people came forward and said, "Me too."

And some of us, regrettably, said to them, "No, that didn't happen to you. No, that's not how it went. No, you didn't have to deal with that. No, it wasn't that difficult. No, you misinterpreted. No, your opportunities are the same as everyone else's. No. No. No."

And we retraumatized those who were doing what they could to be brave.

"We need you to say we matter," they said. And so many said, "Well, don't you think it's better to say that everyone matters?" All this does is perpetuate trauma. Three simple words could have provided an incredible balm. But so many of us refused to say these words. They are, simply, "I believe you."

I believe that what I have experienced and what you have experienced might be different. I believe you when you say you are scared. I believe you when you say you are tired. I believe you when you say you are heartbroken. I believe you when you say you are grieving. I believe you.

The Irish poet Pádraig Ó Tuama taught me that the Irish word *scáth* can mean both "shelter" and "shadow."[2] He says that what one person may see as a shelter, another may see as a shadow, and vice versa. What protects one of us may bully or overtake another of us.

Other words for *shadow*:	Other words for *shelter*:
dominate	protect
eclipse	cover
minimize	defend
reduce	sanctuary
harm	refuge

As you can see, these are two very different experiences, and I believe this is more than just language, more than just wordplay. What some of us see as comfort and safety others of us will experience as threat and even danger.[3]

Can we admit this to ourselves and each other? Can we say, yes, it is possible that the very thing I have experienced as a shelter, you have experienced as a shadow? Could we start there? Hope for reconciliation begins with empathy because empathy subverts the *us vs. them* paradigm. It begins with saying that I can allow space for the fact that my experience and your experience could be vastly different. And I believe you when you tell me what it's been like for you.

After loving our own people and practicing some subversive empathy, the next thing that I believe will heal the world comes to us by way of these disruptive words from Saint Augustine:

Hope has two beautiful daughters; their names are Anger and Courage. Anger at the way things are, and Courage to see that they do not remain as they are.[4]

Our hope gives birth to anger because we see things that abuse the eternity God set in our hearts.[5] We see the lack of dignity given to our brother or sister. We see the vulnerable being victimized. We see the sacred being mocked. It should anger us. It's a violation of our God-image.

Our hope also gives birth to courage because we know, deeply, that our participation matters. This is a kind of prophetic hope. It sees what is not-yet and believes that this not-yet might just be possible. It invites us to look at where we've been given favor, influence, and a voice, and then invites us to participate.

What angers you? What injustice do you see that needs your attention, that gnaws at you, that taps on your shoulder, that invites you?

These expressions of hope are not reserved for politicians, pastors, or people standing on giant platforms. These expressions of hope start right here, in our living rooms, in our minivans, in our park playdates, in our social media feeds, in our dinnertime conversations, in the time we take to stand up and speak out, and in the time we take to listen and learn.

Prophetic hope says that the bridge has already been built. Through Christ, reconciliation has happened. Our reconciliation not just with God but with each other. It is already there. The bridge is already constructed.

To be clear, I am talking about the Christ who was constantly being baited toward a rhetorical trap, toward black-and-white law, toward them/us divisions, and who stood up— EVERY SINGLE TIME—to that religiosity. He chose people over the law. He chose people and their pain over the pressure of the party line, the church rules. You cannot read the New Testament and ignore this.

The path to each other is obscured by our fear. It is only when we examine our own hearts and our own lives that the clouds begin to dissipate and we see that the bridge was there all along. It is then that we can take the first true step toward our brother, our sister, ourselves, God. We may not be able to see the entire bridge all at once. But we can see the first step, then the next, then the next. It is not someone else's responsibility to search my heart. It is not my responsibility to search someone else's heart. It is my responsibility to search my own heart.

Don't assume that anger and courage are only the work of the literal sword. They are the dissident work of the poet, the mother, the teacher, the gardener. They are the disruptive work of the listener, the darkness-dweller, the prophet, the mystic. And they are the work we have all been called to as agents of reconciliation. So, let us all, in the name of hope and her two beautiful daughters, take at least a few minutes in our own quiet hearts and ask God where he may want us in this fight. And then, let us brandish the specific weapons we have been given to enact justice in our world.

What is your weapon? We've each been given something. A thing we can choose to pay attention to, nurture, put into action. A gift, skill, perspective, or way of being that would help us if we gave it away to others who need it too. Maybe there were years we got away from it, covered it up, or felt like it wasn't enough or couldn't possibly be our thing. But I think we are most at home when we come back to this God-given gift. We know it was given to us, so it feels like an act of generosity to give it away.

Finally, I love what Pulitzer Prize–winning poet Jericho Brown adds:

Hope is always accompanied by the imagination, the will to see what our physical environment deems impossible. Only the creative mind can make use of hope. Only a creative people can wield it.[6]

Only the creative among us can wield hope. It requires an imaginative seeing, a kind of resourceful showing up. I absolutely love this because it challenges me. Am I being creative in my hope? Am I thinking beyond the four sides of the box, am I asking good questions, am I asking God to open my eyes?

This reminds me of a conversation God and I had years ago, a conversation that anchors every one of these pages:

Leeana: God, what wonder do you see in me?

God: Hope. Hope is a part of your wonder. You are not a cynic. You are a believer. You believe people can heal. You believe beauty matters. You believe creating matters. You believe things could change. You believe the Chargers can win the Super Bowl, for crying out loud. This is all hope.

Leeana: God, how do I cultivate hope?

God: You use your hopeful voice. Don't edit it. Don't apologize for it. Don't downplay it. Don't silence it.[7]

So that's what I'm doing, my friends. The best that I can. I am using my hopeful voice to love my people. I am using my hopeful voice to extend abundant empathy. I am using my hopeful voice to express anger and to choose courage. And I am using my hopeful voice imaginatively, to offer ideas of how I think things can be, even as we walk through how things are.

I believe in the possibility of healing. And I believe it begins with me.

HOLDING HOPE

God, what do you want to say to me about starting small, empathy, anger and courage, and imagination?

19

hope

IN CROSSING OVER

anyway

> Let us go across to the other side.
>
> —Mark 4:35 ESV

I ASKED LINSEY if she would send me a "retreat box" for my birthday last year. Not only is Linsey one of my Warrior Sisters, but she is also a spiritual director and an overall red-phone-to-Jesus kind of gal. I told her that when my kids were with their dad, I wanted to spend some time doing a one-day personal retreat, and I wanted her to design it for me.[1]

So she did. And it was nothing short of revelatory. For one portion of the retreat, I was to choose my own adventure, and she had included some different options for that portion of the day. I was immediately drawn to a full-color printout of Rembrandt's 1633 painting *Storm on the Sea of Galilee*, which is a rendering of Jesus in the boat with the disciples during the storm. I looked at the instructions for this exercise.

First, I was to read through the story in Mark 4:35–41 in the New Testament several times, paying attention to a word or phrase that I was drawn to.

In the story of Jesus calming the wind and the waves, the author begins by saying that Jesus and the disciples got in the boat in the first place because they needed to go across to the other side. It was in that crossing over from one side to the other that the storm blew up out of nowhere, threatening their vessel and their lives.

Two seconds into the reading, right there in this idea of crossing over, I found myself. From one shore to the other. From the old country to the new country. Anytime we are crossing over, from one point of orientation to another point of reorientation, we typically must travel through vast disorientation. And disorientation is stormy. This does not seem like a foreign concept, but it was there on the page, a reminder, a source of comfort. **Sometimes we need the storms to be normalized so that we don't buy into the belief that we could have avoided the rough waters if only we had navigated better.**

I underlined "Let us go across to the other side" with the hot-pink pen Lins had provided.

The major issue for the men in the story was that Jesus— the person who had a shot at helping them in the middle of this storm—was asleep. The men on the boat shook him awake, likely feeling abandoned in their suffering. He said these few words: *Peace. Be still.*

The wind and the waves obeyed him, and there was a "great calm."

Next, Linsey instructed, I was to look at Rembrandt's painting. I was to look closely at each of the men in the boat and find myself in one of their faces, one of their postures.

Who am I in this picture? Who am I in the storm? There are fourteen men on the boat. Jesus, his twelve disciples, and an extra. The extra, and we are not sure which man is considered the extra, is thought to be Rembrandt himself, my notes tell me. Historically, Rembrandt was known to paint himself somewhere into all his paintings.

According to Linsey's notes, I was to go through each of the faces on the boat. One by one. I was given a description of every single person on the boat. Half of the painting is light-filled and the other half of the painting is darker. More than half the men in the picture are on this calmer, darker side of the boat. They are in various postures near Jesus.

The other half are on the brighter side of the boat in various states of chaos and concern. I saw the man who is closest to the edge of the boat, holding on desperately, taking the waves straight to the face, his mouth wide open, gaping and gasping. *Yep*, I thought. *That looks familiar*. This man looked overwhelmed, barely able to hang on.[2]

I put stars by him with the turquoise pen Lins provided.

Why do some of us choose to stand at the crest of the wave, taking it in the face, fighting for all we're worth, futilely and for no good reason? Pounding the waves with our fists.

My immediate familiarity with this man told me that I do this. I stand at the edge of the crisis and I get into my fighting stance. I raise my fists and I steel my gaze and I work.

Aspects of this stance have served me: strength, resilience, courage, fortitude. But now I'm tired. And I look to the other side of the boat and I see so many others sitting by Jesus, seemingly expending far less physical and emotional energy. Somewhere along the way, Jesus was no longer speaking to the storm, he was speaking to me. *Peace. Be still.*

145

I think those three words were meant as much for the men in the boat as they were for the storm. Or maybe they were entirely for the men in the boat, but the wind and the waves just happened to overhear.

When I see the man in the painting trying to assert his will against the water, the futility is so obvious. The only things that are going to help in this situation are the things that always help and the things we tend to think of last.

Breathe. Admit you are powerless and you need help from a Higher Power, a source outside yourself. Remember that this admission IS your power. We stop trying to use our big brains and brawn to solve our problems and instead we go from plan to posture.

Lie flat on your back. Hands at your sides. Palms up. Begin to breathe slowly and deeply. "Here I am. I'm choosing surrender. I'm choosing to listen. I will cease striving. I am putting my will in corpse pose. I am putting my engine in corpse pose. I am putting my big brain and my great ideas and my strategic acumen in corpse pose."

The storm is absolutely inevitable. And the tendency, my tendency anyway, is to beat my fists at the water. Take it in the face. Flail.

At some point we will be gasping and choking and spluttering and drenched, and we will look around and realize that nothing much has changed. The storm is still raging and we are losing ground despite all our various efforts. It's OK. We will each fight the way we need to fight. But I think we all know, somewhere deep inside, that no matter how skilled we are at fighting, no matter how much tolerance we've built up to suffering, no matter how much we can bench-press, we don't actually have control over the storm.

It's not ever going to be all up to us.

It is at this point that we might want to consider a break from taking it in the face. It is at this point that we might want to consider peace; be still.

One of the things Linsey pointed out to me later is that the disciples knew Jesus as teacher. But after they witnessed his voice calm the wind and the waves, they saw him as God. This experience in the storm expanded their view of him. So it has been in my own storm.

If you are in a season of crossing over, from orientation to reorientation, you have inevitably experienced the frustration, maybe even panic, of disorientation. You might have wondered if God is completely absent in your struggle. And if not absent, then perhaps impotent. I understand the temptation to want to assume that it's always going to feel the way it does right now and that there is no way out.

Maybe God's words to me will serve as some comfort to you: *This is tumultuous. This is what it takes to cross over. I will not let the storm consume you. You are not going to perish. We are not lost. This is not a mistake. I did not fall asleep and lose control of a situation. You have not been forgotten. Peace. Be still.*

HOLDING HOPE

God, what do you want to say to me about "peace; be still"?

20

hope
IN ENDINGS
anyway

A place belongs forever to whoever claims it hardest, remembers it most obsessively, wrenches it from itself, shapes it, renders it, loves it so radically that he remakes it in his own image.

—Joan Didion

THE FIRST SIX MONTHS after moving from San Diego to Lynchburg, I didn't return to California at all. But I would go back and forth four times over the following six months. And it was all goodbyes.

Sometimes it can feel like if you go back to the former place, it will threaten everything you are trying to establish and secure in the new place. But at some point you have to find some kind of way to integrate the past and the present, I believe. And so, when it was time, I did that.

I went to the house, what had been our house, alone. It was finally ready to go on the market, and so it was time to say goodbye. I walked every room, every inch, the entire acre-plus of land. I cried a whole bucket of tears. I thought about my kids on the huge prehistoric rocks—"the dinosaurs," they called them—with popsicles, the hours in the pool, the crib against the wall in the girls' room, the fountain in the courtyard, the rustle of wind through the palms almost every hour of every day, the two four-year-olds and the one-year-old we had brought home to this place. I thought about the words I wrote there and the prayers I prayed there.

I walked past the place where my desk used to sit, the back patio where one million meaningful conversations had taken place with people we loved. Our bedroom. The living room with the wood-burning fireplace, my favorite feature of the entire house. The pots of bougainvillea—some thriving, some withering. Luke's room and the small table he used to showcase our LEGO creations.

I said, "Thank you for holding us, for receiving us when we were tired and limping a bit. Thank you for the celebrations here, the space and time to enjoy so many important people. Thank you for your beauty and for your safety."

I also remembered the strain, the impossible conversation at the dining room table, the loss too. Honestly, I was heartbroken. And sometimes the only way to tolerate heartbreak is to walk right into the living room of our loss.

We landed at that house after a two-year military tour in the Middle East that had been cut short due to unexpected new orders. We had three kids ages four and under, and we had been in a place during a time that required high vigilance. We were ready to give our nervous systems a break. As we walked through customs on our way back into San Diego, we were already in escrow on this old Spanish house that sat on a hill. We were ready for a place of our own.

We were there only four years, but they were formative years. I still miss the house. Some days I can feel that place in my body, as though the places where we lived and breathed and inhabited also inhabit us, take up space in us, breathe in us. I think Lomita Road will always be like that for me.

I was scrolling through pictures with Elle the other day, and there it was—a picture of the house. I enlarged it and then closed it again. Have you ever loved something or someone so much and also had this sense that you couldn't get away fast enough? It's almost too tender to look at. Too tender to touch. You have to move away from it for fear it will break your heart all over again.

I needed a way to think about this loss. A way arrived. The voice said, *Just because it's over doesn't mean it's gone*. I needed to hear that because it seemed as though the previous fifteen years had completely evaporated. Or that they were years I was supposed to forget or erase or regret. But that didn't seem right either. Those years were part of my life. Those years gave me my children. Those years took us on countless adventures and gave us unparalleled experiences. Those years were a very real part of what has brought me to today.

I decided to honor our time at that house, our years together, our memories. This ritual of walking through the rooms, thanking each part and place, was an important exercise in gratitude and in closure.

If you've had to say goodbye to something, I hope you've been able to find a way to bring the good of it with you too. I know it might seem simpler to just completely eliminate the past, but I think life calls for a bit more nuance than that.

The invitation I received was to expand, not erase. We don't eradicate the past; we enlarge in order to accommodate both what has been and what is and what will be.

Instead of having contempt or disgust or anger or regret, I return to gratitude. It's the only thing that makes sense. Everything else gets so lodged in me, turns so toxic, that I risk losing what I have now, what is in front of me today. And, again, I don't think we have that kind of time.

Why is an ending worthy of our hope? How is an ending hopeful at all? "It is finished," Jesus breathed from the cross. It is done, complete. There is no rising without the grave. So, I guess I find slivers of hope in endings because, if we will name them and honor them, they are actually where the new beginning begins.

If you are facing an ending of any kind, could you take a moment to walk into the middle of it and say thank you and goodbye? Thank you for holding me then, for bringing me to where I am now, for the memories I will always have. Thank you. And goodbye. Goodbye to what was and to what could have been. Goodbye.

Goodbye, Lomita Road. Thank you for holding us until it was time to let us go.

HOLDING HOPE

God, what do you want to say to me about
"Thank you and goodbye"?

21

hope

IN THE WILDERNESS

anyway

I am going to do something new.
It is already happening. Don't you recognize it?
I will clear a way in the desert.
I will make rivers on dry land.

—Isaiah 43:19 GW

IN-BETWEEN IS HARD. Really hard. Middles are messy. Moving from what was to what will be is protracted.

It is hard to talk about and write about these times when we are in them because we are, well, *in them*. And these spaces require all that we have in order to accomplish basic functioning. Some might refer to this as "survival mode."

In survival mode, we tend to have distorted vision. We look back with fondness on things that weren't particularly fond. Or maybe we tell ourselves how horrible it all was and how glad we are it's done. We might also look forward to an unknown future, sure of solutions that will deliver us onto preferable footing. Or we despise our future, sure that nothing could possibly come from our losses. We are not where we were, and we are not yet where we are going. And there is very little about the displacement that we like. Nothing about disorientation deeply resonates with the human spirit.

The wilderness is a long stretch of "ifs" that we are thrust into because of loss or change, so it's very difficult for us to internalize this stretch as anything other than challenging, maybe even futile. I have spent a lot of time trying to figure out how to truncate the wilderness, how to move it along so I don't have to tolerate it any longer. But that's missing the point, I think. The point is that the wilderness is what it takes to go from the old country to the new country. And it takes what it takes.

The thing I've always loved about the idea of the wilderness is that the word means "wild place." Anything can happen in the wild place—anything can grow, anything can arrive, anything can die, anything can be lost, anything can be found. In this way, the wilderness is always generative, if you think about it. It always produces *something*, even if that something is acceptance.

In the wilderness, we find sustenance in very unexpected places. In the wilderness, we confront ourselves and our greatest fears. In the wilderness, we find benevolence. In the wilderness, we find others who are also there, on similar journeys. In the wilderness, we find our priorities. In the wilderness, we begin to understand loss. In the wilderness, we find our humanity; we are invited to welcome our vulnerability, which will guide us to the gift we are to give away to the world.

This is why every great journey involves a wilderness. We often have to experience the great expanse of nothing in order to understand anything.

> Before you know what kindness really is
>> You must lose things.
>>>>> —Naomi Shihab Nye[1]

Last summer, my group gathered for two nights in a split-level home perched way up in the cliffs of Point Loma in San Diego. We gathered from Montana and New York and Virginia and Colorado and California. We gathered on the absolute eve of sending one of our own off on a foreign service tour in Oman. We gathered the large net that we have become and have stretched beneath each other, and we celebrated.

One night a few of us were still up late, and one of our dear beloveds was saying she was lost, that she felt like she was losing herself under the weight of tragedy and trauma that continued to descend on her and her family. She wasn't exaggerating. The list is so long and so loud that you would not believe it if I typed it all here for you to read. She has been buried over and over and over again. Asked to enter the wilderness over and over and over again.

She was crying. And let me tell you that she has earned every tear. And those of us who were up with her, witnessing her pain, were crying too. She was reduced, her eyes were flat, she was losing the fight and light that are both so often in her. She was fading right before us, traces of her spark already gone.

This happens. We are just so solidly exhausted by the demands of the wilderness, we are so aware that any kind of relief is simply a mirage, and we are acquainted with our own dislocation so severely that we begin to dim. Hope begins to dim.

I looked hard into her face, trying to find that trace of fire way back in the recesses of her aquamarine eyes, and I told her what the voice had told me one hundred times over the previous two years: "You are not consumed." I took her hand, I looked at her in the way that you look at someone when you want them to know you really see them, and I said again, "You are not consumed."

"It's not possible," I told her. "Because of God's great love for you, you are not consumed. I know it feels like it. I know it feels like you are losing yourself and this fight and your footing and your way. But, and this is extremely important, you are not consumed. You will not be annihilated by this. It is not possible. There is a great love for you that will not allow it."[2]

There's something about hearing this from a fellow wilderness wanderer. There's something about hearing these words from someone who is also in the thick of losing the light. It does not ring as true when someone yells it down from the mountaintop.

In recovery, the acronym for HOPE is

H earing
O ther
P eople's
E xperiences

I told her how I had turned this phrase into a breath prayer: *Because of God's great love* (on the inhale), *I am not consumed* (on the exhale). It is a rare and gracious gift to have these words to breathe and remember. Especially when we are feeling like we are completely and totally done for.

I can look back on the last three years and see tiny pinholes of illuminated ground, one after another, tiptoeing through the wilderness, like a Morse code of dots and dashes that make their way across an austere landscape. The language of grace. Lily pads, stepping-stones, railroad ties, bushwhacked trails. Call them what you want but know that you can't usually see them until you look back. All you have right now is the one you're standing on and the faintest outline of the one on its way.

I can also see the mighty James River, running parallel to Imperial Tobacco Lofts, stretching north as far as my view would go, respite in the dry lands. Remember that no matter how impossible today feels, no matter how disoriented you seem, God makes streams in the desert for his people. He does new things. He accompanies us with such stunning creativity. Because of his great love for you, you are not consumed.

If the middle that you're in is particularly messy, if the wilderness feels interminable, if the teeth of the unknown are gnawing at you, read the following. Read it out loud as a blessing over your life and your story.

This is the way God put it:

> "They found grace out in the desert,
>> these people who survived the killing.
> Israel, out looking for a place to rest,
>> met God out looking for them!"
> God told them, "I've never quit loving you and never
> will.
>> Expect love, love, and more love!

And so now I'll start over with you and build you up
     again,
         dear virgin Israel.
You'll resume your singing,
     grabbing tambourines and joining the dance."[3]

My hope is built on nothing less: God has never quit loving
you and never will.

HOLDING HOPE

God, what do you want to say to me
about "You are not consumed"?

22

hope
IN RADICAL
ACCEPTANCE
anyway

God comes to you disguised as your life.

—Richard Rohr

THE THING I'M TRYING TO INTERNALIZE these days is that I'm OK. I have spent too much time telling myself I've missed it, neglected it, ignored it, forgotten it, or wasted it. It = how to do life. This kind of self-assessment sends me to Crazy Town. So I have to sit down and breathe and remind myself that I'm OK. Because the feelings of "not OK" threaten everything—my equanimity and balance and breath and presence and, yes, my capacity for anything resembling hope.

Why, after I have spent so much time planning, purchasing, trying, trying, trying, am I sitting here typing this and the new rug under the couch smells like dog pee? I replaced the former rug—that is now in my garage—because *it* smelled like dog pee. Why does everything SMELL LIKE PEE?

There's a long white extension cord that hangs from the back of my one-ton TV—which is mounted on the wall—down to an outlet five feet away. It is so aesthetically perverse that it makes me angry daily. There's an outlet behind the TV, on the wall, but it will take three grown people to take the TV off the wall, reach behind, and plug it back in, while a person is holding both sides of the TV, and then remount it. This will also require two ladders or, at the very least, step stools. I don't have three grown people and I don't have ladders.

There is an infestation of large black ants that are coming from somewhere. I don't know where. I have ant traps on my list. Please don't get me started about my list.

The pilot light went out on the gas fireplace a couple of weeks ago. Normally, I've been able to relight it myself, but this time I can't get it going. I try, but then I get scared that I'm going to blow my face off and I stop trying.

Three of the five burners on my range are not working properly. My vacuum fell over and took a nice-sized chunk, in a visible area, out of the wood floor: a white scar right there in the middle of the walkway. The countertop cracked in one area. The front door won't lock, all of a sudden. The internet is spotty at best.

I really do try. I'm not over here attempting to see how far I can let things go. I am relatively on it, and I don't particularly enjoy the scent of canine urine. At all. It's not like this is how I want things to be, how I want to live, and yet, here we are.

My own personal tendency is to judge my overwhelm as failure.

Maybe one reason why this gets stuck inside me is that it *is*, partly, at least, true. If I had a different set of life skills, a different personality, a different perspective, a different set of circumstances, a different bank account . . . perhaps things would be different. But there is no amount of fixating that will change one thing.

This is the life I have, and the home I have, and the kids I have, and the marital status I have, and the bank account I have, and the work I have, and the calves I have, and the dog (give me strength) I have. This is the life I have been given, the life I accept with gratitude.

But I'm tired. I'm tired of making lists and making calls and making messes.

How do I make peace with ant invasions and pet urine?

How do I make peace with derelict burners and countertop cracks?

How do I make amends with this body, this SHE that is only ever asking for love?

How do I find any capacity whatsoever to remain present in my own life when these things are constantly swirling around me?

I just walked from the couch to the bathroom and passed seven cords, unplugged, sticking out, waggling at me. Hair tools, fan, diffuser, chargers. The more I count, the more they start to feel like snakes all coming for me, closing in, constricting. Do you have these thoughts too?

I want to be the kind of mom who _____.

I want to be the kind of housekeeper who _____.

I want to be the kind of woman who _____.

God, I can't find you in this. I can't hear you in the swirl of it all.

Once again, the voice says, *Leeana, your person is you. How you are. Who you are. Where you are. As you are. Your person is you.*

My eyes fill with tears because there is some kind of relief in these words. A vote of confidence, perhaps. The rug and the cords and the burners don't get the last word. You are where you were meant to be. You are who you were meant to be. Right now. Even with all this. You get to claim your one precious self.

This is what you've been given. Sorrow? Peace? Tragedy? Heartbreak? Urine? This is what you've been given. Stand still. Stiller. Stiller yet. This right here is what you have been given. Do not try to scan the horizon for a magic apple. Do not listen to the silky voices that will tell you it's better somewhere else, that you don't have to feel whatever this is.

The Great Secret is this: where you are right now—right now—is the most mattering thing. What we go through trying to hush reality. What great lengths and attempts and stutter steps we try to pull off doing anything we can to avoid standing right here.

It's hard, I tell God. It's hard to lean up against the chaos, internally and externally, every day. It's hard to know what needs my attention and what doesn't and what deserves my time and what doesn't and what I should do and what I should get help with or try to hire out. I swirl like this a lot.

And I can feel the swirl in my body—in my jaw, my shoulders, my eyes. I want to jump out of my skin, but of course the invitation is radical acceptance. Breathe into the places that are tight. Listen.

I lay my head back against the couch and I breathe for a bit. Tears thicken. I'm so frustrated. I'm so freaking frustrated.

I am tired of trying and things always being in half-repair or disrepair. I'm tired of giving everything I have and it not mattering.

And I realize I am no longer talking to myself about the house. I am talking about my life. My work. My mothering. About all the things I take seriously and personally that I wish I felt I was better at.

Then I get a text from my sister. She and my niece Lindsay want to stop in for a visit sometime today.

The whisper in my ear is this: radical acceptance.

Radical acceptance of my life, my marital status, my disappointment, my frustration, even the dog. Radical acceptance of this reality, this place, this body. The cords, the burners, the ants, the divot in the floor.

Hello, chaos. I cannot outrun you. No matter how fast I get. No matter who I hire. No matter if I buy new. Hello. You want to take me away from myself, pull me out to sea. You want to disintegrate me and fragment me into a million pieces. Hello, you. I see you.

And hello, self. I see you in all your intricacies and nuances. I see you wanting to create and nurture and nourish. And I see you wanting some small semblance of order in which to do that. I see you wanting perfection sometimes too. Wanting it all to look exactly right. I see you wishing for that, trying to create that, longing for it, actually. I want to take you by the hand and help you walk into what is. Not what I wish for in my fantasy of perfectionism. What is.

Go find God in the cords. Go find God in the crumbs under the bed. Go find God in the ants. Go find God in the frustration, disappointment, chaos. Go find God. This is your only hope.

My sister says, "We are going through the drive-through on our way over. Can we bring you a tea? We are going to the dump after we leave your house. Can we take the boxes in the garage for you? We can help you with the TV cord. No prob."

Yes, I say. Yes. I will accept this miracle too.

HOLDING HOPE

God, what do you want to say to me
about radical acceptance?

23

hope
IN WHAT BROUGHT
YOU HERE
anyway

The way forward always in the end
The way that you came.

—David Whyte

NOT LONG AGO, the voice whispered this simple phrase to me: *What brought you here will take you forward.* It was at a particularly whipped-up point when this simple phrase arrived. *What brought you here will take you forward.* And at first, I was a tiny bit indignant.

What brought me here? Let me tell you what brought me here! Heartbreak, loss, reduction, the very things I never wanted. Obviously, these are not the kinds of companions I want to take forward with me. Duh.

I spent eighteen weeks in the early part of 2019 in a divorce recovery group. It was humbling and odd and beautiful, as I believe most recovery groups are. There was a man in a V-neck powder-yellow cashmere sweater who assuaged his loneliness by driving for Uber. A woman whose estranged husband was in jail for indescribable acts. It was unexpectedly healing to be in a room with these people and their stories.

One of the weeks, we talked about grief and loss, and we were asked to make an inventory of all our losses as a result of the divorce. So, not just the loss of the primary relationship but all the loss-tentacles that reached and wound and stretched into areas of our lives we didn't even realize had been touched.

More than just about anything from those eighteen weeks, I remember that one exercise, that one question, because it summed up so much of the experience of the previous months and years. It made me realize how much loss accompanies loss, and so I felt a bit salted right in the wound when the voice offered this cool-cat phrase. *What brought you here will take you forward.*

You know what got me here, I said, and it's been nothing but hard.

True. But what else? What brought you **here***? Was it, possibly, courage? Resilience? Love for your children and love for your family? Your Warrior Sisters? Hope in the future? Is it possible that those are the things that brought you here?*

(Um, shut up.)

What brought you here, Leeana, to this exact place where you are standing are all the very same things that are going to take you forward. So, get real familiar with the ragtag resources you've got. They've been your companions up to this point, and they will be your companions still.

This seemed important and perhaps even true, so I began to make an inventory—a winding inventory—of what got me here besides the sadness, the heartbreak. What about the hope? What about the perseverance? What about the re-building? And what about the people—the gorgeous, brilliant people who held me, carried me, continue to hold me up? Didn't they get me here too?

What brought you here will take you forward.

Is it possible that the things we've leaned on so heavily in order to get to today are still with us? Still available? Still running to our side?

A few days ago I had about an hour and a half in the car alone. I had been able to feel the anxiety in my throat the entire day prior. Anxiety about deadlines and responsibili-ties and what school was going to look like this year and the way I wanted to do things but the way I can't seem to ever get them done.

I turned on a podcast and then promptly turned it off. I knew what I needed, so I started talking out loud as I drove.

"I'm here," I said. "I'm frustrated and overwhelmed and totally unable to focus. I'm blind with inefficiency. I guess I'm just not very good at my own life."

And when I said those last words, the tears came rolling down my cheeks. When things are hard—even things that I have no control over, like a pandemic—I always assume I've missed something. And if I could just figure out what I'm missing, what I'm not getting, the appropriate system or solution, all will be well. But, of course, I can't because—as we've established—I'm just not very good at my own life.

Hot tip: If you ever hear yourself say a sentence like this out loud in a silent car, you might want to take that as a sign that you've somehow lost the plot a teensy, tiny bit. You might want to consider that you need a nap.

Well, there it is, I thought. That's the thorn that stuck in my soul: *I guess I'm just not very good at my own life.*

Who told you that? the voice said. *Where did you get that data?*

And we talked it out. About an hour of driving due east and talking out loud in my car and crying, all while chain-chewing bubblemint gum and drinking four sparkling waters.

This has brought me here. This voice. With its timely one-liners and its listening. It has held no matter what. This voice has never left my side. Not for one second.

It has watched over me as I have slept, as I have cried, as I have traveled and journaled and worked and kissed my babies' necks. It has held my hand—viscerally—when I have gone out into the night air after everyone else is asleep and cried. It has followed me into the woods behind my house and outside when I was walking Rosie at the Lofts. It is present when I'm packing lunches and when I'm paying bills. Over and over again, the voice has brought me the *something* that I could not have procured on my own.

I could not ditch this voice if I tried. Like allergies or glitter or freckles or a stray cat or your shadow, this voice remains.

What else brought you here?

What is your inventory? What brought you to this moment? What brought you here, to this place? What brought you to your geographical setting? What brought you to your current home, your current body, your current work? What brought you to this inner landscape, where your heart is now, where your mind is now? What brought you to this exact place? Where you are standing. Where you are thinking. Where you are feeling. Where you are resting. Where you are troubled. Where you are confused. Where you are loved.

Why does it matter what brings us to certain moments? Is it chance? Decisions could have gone a thousand different ways and things would look entirely different. Decisions I made. Decisions others made that have affected me. Decisions I made in response to other people's decisions.

I want to know—like you do, perhaps—that I haven't messed it all up. I want to know that somehow the sum of all of these decisions matters. And that what has brought us here is all important and valuable. Not only what has brought us here, but the fact that it all brought us *here*, to this place.

Maybe we're all longing to hear this: that the path that brought us here was not meaningless. Our interpretation of the signs along the way was good enough. Our love for those we are journeying with surpasses any of the horrible mistakes we might have made unintentionally.

Sometimes we have to leave where we've been. Because where we've been is no longer. And where we have to go is—in its starting over—fiercely new. Even if you are returning to the tiny town where you went to college, your new self and your new story make it all an untraveled frontier.

You are being asked to trust that you will find what you need in the new country. The new country is where you are called to go, and the only way to go there is naked and vulnerable. Risk a few more steps into the new country, trusting that each time you enter it, you will feel more comfortable and be able to stay longer.

—Henri Nouwen, *The Inner Voice of Love*[1]

What will we eat? When will we arrive in the promised land? At least back there we knew where our next meal was coming from. We don't appreciate the dis-ease, but in order to become ourselves we could not—for some reason—remain in the "back there" of our story. We had to come forward. We had to move further into the landscape.

It is OK to travel into the next new moment. It is OK to leave what was. It is OK to fight for yourself. It is OK to say, "I need to move on from here. This place is bones and I need flesh." It is OK to allow a path to be made. It is OK to take the path, to get up, to walk on. You are allowed to walk on. Even though you will leave precious, precious things behind.

Running away is never, in the history of ever, a solution. But moving forward, moving toward and into—even if it is into a desert or wilderness—is sometimes the truest path to take.

What if we messed it all up? What if you did? What if I did? What if we could have done better? When I am tired and sad, I am plagued by these questions.

The trees in my backyard are bare. It's February and they have been stick-figured for a couple of months now. Even the leaves that were once on them have washed away in the rain. In December, I lay down on the leaves like a mulchy mattress, and they were so thick that I had to burrow into them to even touch the ground beneath. Now they are gone. Washed away by rain, I guess. Decomposed, perhaps. What happens to all those leaves?

Through the stand of spindled tree trunks, I see a floor of red dirt where the leaves had been. Almost like a large red skating pond. My own little red sea that continues—all these thousands of years later—to part. Not all in one grand swoosh, of course. But infinitesimally, a dry place appears, just as I need to set my foot.

Some days the footing is far soggier than I'd prefer. And that red dirt is invasive, so no matter how hard I try to keep it outside, it is in my grout and on the sheets and dish towels and on the bottom of every sock we own. It looks like someone has come in and doused Frank's Hot Sauce erratically and everywhere. What in the actual *bleeeeeeeep*?

We bring the ground with us where we go.

I see some poetry in this now, maybe. The path that brought me here is the same path that will lead me on.

Here are the things on that path:

Love for my children.

Love for my family.

Love for my circle of trust.

Love for words and making them into things.

Love for laughing.

Love for finding meaning and beauty laced throughout
     this world.

Today, I step on, I walk on, I live on. I will make sausage-and-kale soup in a bit. My eyes will sting and run when I cut the onions. I may go outside for some exercise if it's not too cold. If it is too cold, I will do some yoga inside. This all assumes my mental health holds between now and then. If it doesn't, I will nap.

The morning will go too quickly, and just like that, I will be out the door to pick up kids from school and our afternoon will commence. At some point, I will likely need to fold the clean laundry that is covering the couch. I will need to serve the soup and think through Elle's eighth birthday party this weekend.

Yesterday I got the news that a dear friend's breast biopsy was clear. The day before that I got a picture of my brother holding my brand-new baby nephew, and I could barely swallow the knot in my throat for the joy of those two.

This afternoon, I may get a call from my sister. There's an audiobook I borrowed from the library that I want to pass on to her. I will help Lane and her friend work on their science project together. I will make a list of the things I want to get done this week, about half of which will actually happen.

This evening, I will lay out my outfit for the gym tomorrow. I will take out the trash. I will ask my mom if she can get Luke from school tomorrow. I will mindlessly handle the round medal that hangs around my neck. The cross of St. Benedict. An ancient monk who whispered in my ear over a decade ago, "Always we begin again." Tonight, I will grade essays from my English 101 students.

Tomorrow I will do a radio interview and then take kids to after-school activities. I will take my Wellbutrin in the morning and my Lexapro at night, like I always do. I will drink as much coffee as my body will allow. I'll light the fireplace.

I will look up. At least once. And say thank you.

HOLDING HOPE

*God, what do you want to say to me
about what brought me here?*

24

hope
IN YOUR ROOTS
anyway

Smile, breathe and go slowly.

—Thich Nhat Hanh

LAST OCTOBER, my friend Elaine and I hosted an intimate women's retreat at her family property on Orcas Island, Washington.[1] Most everything about the weekend was perfect: the women, the setting, the food. Ugh, the food. Just six short months after, we were in total lockdown due to the pandemic, and so the time spent together in the woods and on the water became that much more sacred retroactively.

We welcomed women from all over the country, all over the age spectrum, all over the spiritual landscape, and we stayed in the room with each other, laughed, cried, walked, wrote, and confided. It was spectacular.

One especially meaningful offering that Elaine proposed was a practice called forest bathing, which is simply intentionally receiving the benefits of everything living in the forest.[2] Creation as a healing agent. I was in. Basically, we would take the women on a short hike up into the more remote areas where there were two ponds and a tiny little hunting cabin and stands and stands of trees covered in moss and lichen, like fairy kisses. I am not kidding you. It is this magical.

Prior to the retreat, Elaine learned a bit about forest bathing, and we set out to offer these women an experience in immersing themselves in what the trees and water and air had to give them. We walked in a line, Elaine in front and me in back. Eighteen women stretched between us. Whispering at times, pointing here or there, stooping down to pick up leaves, but mostly silent. Every so often Elaine stopped and read a piece by Rumi or Thich Nhat Hanh or relayed general information about the forest.

"One mature tree's oxygen output can support 18 people,"[3] she read, which just happened to be the number of attendees we had. But there wasn't just one tree breathing for us all. There were hundreds. Thousands. So, we all breathed deeply, breathing in gratitude for the generosity embedded in the natural world.

Scientists have proven that the forest's root system is one big network of support. Trees can send each other warnings about possible detrimental environmental changes, and the roots of one tree will send nutrients to the roots of another tree that is in need.[4]

What we saw there in the forest was truly beautiful, but it was what we couldn't see that was even more astounding.

We were actually standing on a network filled with hope, a network of mutuality and care.

Once we made it to the top of the climb, the second gorgeous pond revealed itself and the women audibly gasped. Elaine read one more piece, and then we sent the women off to spend some time writing in a nest of their choosing. It was a five-star hotel for the heart.

When I get waaaaaay up into my head, I completely forget that nature exists. I stay inside too long, I only touch synthetic things, I only look at machines. A crazy miracle is waiting for me right outside my door, but I miss it. Until I don't. Maybe that's true of most of us. We forget that the grand elixir, the tonic, the prescription, has already been filled.

I'm sure at least some of the women in attendance were probably like me in that way. Inside too much. Away from nature too long. In need of radical beauty and deep breaths. So, it was of no surprise to me that many of the women, when the weekend was drawing to a close and we were recapping, mentioned the forest bathing as one of the most meaningful components of their weekend—someone forcing them to walk outside, to take in the surroundings, and to sit and write in the woods and then share what surfaced for them during that time.

I look back at that weekend with a kind of awe. At the time, we had absolutely no idea what was coming. We had no idea that the world would shut down, travel would stop, and isolation would mark the next calendar year. I also think about the amount of communication and even a bit of conflict required for Elaine and me to agree on how to bring women from varying backgrounds into the same room. We survived. And I think about the courage of those women to show up and fall open.

Elaine and I walked away with the knowledge that our root system is strong. The network of mutual respect and care and love that we have nurtured together is robust and generous. The hours and hours of listening, loving, and holding each other's losses with tenderness have translated into an enduring symbiosis.

I also witnessed women exposing their own roots. Maybe on varying levels and at different times, but they each, in their own way, said this is what's going on below the surface of my life. This is where the decay has set in. This is where I am depleted. Here's a place I have something extra to give away, and I want to learn how to do that. Here is something I can offer; here is something I need to receive.

We see the surface of most people's lives—the flowering, the flourishing, maybe the decaying. Are there a select few with whom you could join roots and agree to be the kind of people who are allowed to see what's going on under the surface?

I think this is when we do our best work as women. We choose to find our own place in the great network of giving and receiving. We admit our need and we celebrate and offer our resources. We choose to be better together instead of making a name for ourselves as individuals. We choose symbiosis because it makes the entire system stronger.

Elaine and I have often marveled at the fact that we both lost our husbands within about a year of each other. The four of us had spent hours and hours together. We traveled together, celebrated holidays together, became family. But, in what felt like a snap, it all changed. Almost as if those memories were from another life entirely.

What has remained, however, is an unexpected sisterhood that is rooted in both loss and love, in professional respect and personal attachment, and in miles and miles of tunneling toward each other under the surface.

As I write this, the outer rings of Hurricane Isaias are ripping through the woods behind my house. I can almost hear these long, lean ladies yelling back and forth to each other, "OK, girls, let's hunker down. This is a big one. Let's take care of each other. We're in this together."

HOLDING HOPE

God, what do you want to say to
me about my root system?

25

hope
IN WHAT IS NEXT
anyway

The Lord will not forsake his people, for they are his prize.

—Psalm 94:14 TLB

WHAT IS NEXT? This question arrived. I had been telling old stories. Relying on the ones I have known, backward and forward. I was living in very hard spaces, and I wasn't ready to talk about those spaces, and that was OK. The old stories hold us for a time. But then I began to feel tension.

Sometimes we are living in new spaces and new stories, and some part or parts of our life need to catch up. The stories we are living in are no longer large enough to hold who we have become or who we have a sense we are becoming. At some point a threshold will emerge, and that is exactly what happened to me. And so I was asking—or maybe I was asked—*What is next?* This is a profound question.

Where will I spend my time?

Where will I spend my energy?

What will my passion and creativity and curiosity go toward?

What are the new stories I am living?

What are the new stories I want to be telling?

What work, relationships, community, and beliefs are spacious enough to hold who I am becoming?

What is next implies that it is time to leave what has been. It is time for an ending to occur. As we have established, this doesn't mean that what has been is gone. Just because something has ended doesn't mean it has disappeared. The work we've given to a job or career. The time and energy we've given to a relationship. The love we've poured into a neighborhood or community. Just because it's over doesn't mean it's gone. As Anne Lamott says, "The beauty was not lost—it cannot be. All that we gave remains."[1] I think this is right.

But a time comes when it will be clear that the question on the table is "What is next?" And we each have permission, when the time is right, to allow that question to arrive. Welcome it, even. Hope is embedded in this question. You mean there's a next? What a relief.

In my own life, I've often found that I cannot always determine or discern what is next while I'm standing at a safe distance from my life. I have to step into the unknown in order to have the space to hear. We can't always jump from one known to the next known. There is typically a letting go that must occur before we know exactly what we are to take hold of.

If you have an inkling that it is time for *next*, you may have that inkling before you even know what the *next* is. But somehow, you know it is time. This knowing is as important as the actual answer to the question, I think. Knowing that next is coming is significant.

The etymology of the word *next* relates to the word *nigh*. In other words, what is near? What is near to you? What is already in your hands or maybe just a step or two away? What is close by in proximity? What is already in your heart? What is already there in your soul?

What I can see in my own life is that what was next was often there all along, but I just needed the courage to move toward it.

Maybe your next is vocational. Maybe your next is relational. Maybe your next is emotional. Maybe your next is spiritual. Maybe your next is geographic.

With God, there is always a next. The wall in front of us is always being transformed into a door if we will see it as such. Maybe your next involves going backward. Maybe it involves going forward. But be assured there is always a next. There is always a hand reaching toward you. There is always an invitation.

I think the best way to know what is next is to be present in the now. That may sound antithetical. If we can get still in the moment, if we can sink deeper into the now and listen, we just might get the gift of next.

It is the now that gives us the next. When we try to launch too far forward, we lose our footing. We try to go up in our heads and make a plan. I'm here to tell you that this rarely works. We plant our feet firmly in the now, in this moment, in these minutes of stillness and silence, and this is the way that what is coming will begin to arrive. **It is our deep commitment to this moment that helps us discern the next.**

Am I open to what is next, whatever that might be? Are my hands open? Is my heart open? My sense is that next will require vulnerability, a willingness to trust God again, trust myself again.

You might not believe it yet, but there is a next for you. I don't know exactly what it is, when it will come, or how it will happen. But I believe God does. And I believe that what's next will be another way that you experience lavish love.

I am believing that for myself too.

So, if you feel stuck, if you feel like you're a victim of your circumstances, like there is no way out, no choices, could you believe that with God there is always a next? And could you be on the lookout for what might feel spacious? What might accommodate the you that is arriving?

HOLDING HOPE

God, what do you want to say to
me about what is next?

hope
IN EXPANSION
anyway

We are enlarged in the waiting. We, of course,
don't see what is enlarging us. But the longer we
wait, the larger we become, and the more joyful our
expectancy.

—Romans 8:24–25

IT'S OK TO GRIEVE; it's necessary, even. But it's also
OK—no matter the circumstances—to see this imperceptible
gold filling in the cracks, to see the tiniest shaft of light cutting
into the cell you find yourself in. It's OK to know, deeper
than you know anything, that you will rise.

It's OK to hold that secret close to your heart, even to hide
it for a time. It's OK to secretly believe in your own largeness,
your own capacity, your own resilience. It's absolutely OK to
nourish and nurture your true self and not have to do any
explaining.

It's OK to create a culture in your life that echoes this largeness, that assumes you know what you're doing and that supports the doing of it. It's OK to secretly be proud of yourself, to believe that you've done something important, against all odds, even in the face of constant opposition and resistance. Just getting up and living some days is deserving of this kind of self-congratulations.

It's OK to admit that a situation you saw initially as purely reductive has actually brought with it some significant gifts. If we have surrendered to the darkness, if we have spent some time in corpse pose and listened for the voice, if we have allowed it all in, something extraordinary tends to happen: we expand.

This is the hope we have when we are still there in the darkness. Expansion, wings, just might be on their way. And it comes not because of our winning personalities or our amazing strategies or our ability to bypass hardship. It's the opposite. Expansion, true expansion, is typically delivered by the hands of loss. This is the absolute essence of hard-won hope.

We see our circumstances as purely an ending. But remember where we began this conversation: new life starts in the dark. And so our time in the darkness, our time in the grief, our time in the losing, our time in the wilderness, is actually—if we will surrender to it and pay attention while we're there—creating new life. What we see as an ending is also a beginning.

Expansion is not what others have perhaps told us it is or looks like. Expansion is not success, a larger platform, more money, or healthier hair. It's not a more organized home or a developed talent or well-behaved kids. Expansion is nothing about anything on the outside. Expansion is an inside job.

It is the riches that are hand-delivered to the person who will participate in death, burial, and resurrection.

What are these riches? An expansion in our capacity . . .

> to be present with those we love
> to trust the process instead of having to jump ahead and solve
> to trust and listen to our own voice
> to live from abundance instead of fearing scarcity
> to give our work away in the world without apology
> to hold the stories of others
> to grieve our losses instead of numb our pain
> to nourish instead of consume
> to tolerate vulnerability
> to welcome possibility
> to believe in hope anyway
> to reach out for support
> to begin again

This is what we're going to receive, in doses, if we will lie down in the darkness.

We all want someone to tell us how we can take the easy road to a richer inner life. But that's the great lie. The lie says we could experience a depth and maturity and richness, we could experience ourselves and each other and God in a more significant way, by never having to go through anything hard.

We think it's the end. And in some ways, it is. It's the end of what was. But the hard thing is also the seed for the new beginning, and often that new beginning carries with it an opportunity for something truer.

When it's time, when it's finally time to stir and stretch and begin our emergence from the darkness, our prayer is that we will have the courage to step into the new life that is waiting for us. This isn't something we can create on our own. This is the work of God in our life. This is the work of the Spirit. It's soul metamorphosis. I've watched it in others and I've seen it in myself: darkness, surrender, listening, expansion, invitation, emergence, wings.

The secret to expansion, the secret to soul metamorphosis, is loss. And so, if you are in the messy middle of loss, I want you to know there is hope. You are held and loved and seen right where you are, and you are joining a process that will change you from the inside out.

It is OK to let your wings arrive.

HOLDING HOPE

God, what do you want to say
to me about expansion?

27

hope
IN LOVE
anyway

Love never stops loving.

—1 Corinthians 13:8 TPT

AS I'M WRITING THIS FINAL CHAPTER, snow is falling outside. The trees are bare, of course, but enough snow has come down that branches and knots and crooks have all collected a layer of powdered sugar. The harsh edges and ends are softened.

The last big snow like this happened two years ago, when we were living in the Lofts. So I've never really seen these trees, the woods in my backyard, look like this. Narnia suits them. My favorite eight-year-old snoozes next to me as I watch her, type, watch the snow, sip coffee.

In a few short months, it will all change again. The trees will bud and burst, and instead of looking out at white, I will look at a sea of green. A few months after that, fire-kissed reds and oranges and yellows. It will be hard to remember that what I'm looking at right now ever existed.

Growing up in Southern California introduced me to many things, but four distinct seasons was not one of them. Most people might prefer the reliable one-note of San Diego sun, but something in me resonates with the seasons I have found in Central Virginia. Things can and do change, and I guess I've needed to know that.

In her poem "How to Survive This," Barbara Kingsolver writes, "The day will come when I look back amazed."[1]

I brush Elle's hair back from her face and study her profile in the white light. Never neglect the small wonders. Here we are. And though it looks nothing like I had anticipated, it's actually quite beautiful. I am, in fact, amazed.

At the very beginning of our journey together, I said, "The new thing that is being born in you and, therefore, being born into the world, is happening entirely out of love." I've never been more convinced of this.

What if your entire journey has actually been a love letter? What if the last three years of my life have actually been a love letter? A love letter to human resilience and the fights of our lives. A love letter to finding a path through the wilderness, radically accepting our place in the darkness. A love letter to the seasons of our lives, to honor the winters *as much as* the springs.[2] A love letter to all the parts of ourselves we would have never claimed otherwise.

What if love was sitting with me at the dining room table, holding my hand, as that terrible news was delivered? What if love was sitting in that triangle in the therapist's office, following me back to my car, sitting in the passenger seat of my minivan while I opened my hands in surrender to what was happening?

What if love was beside me in the living room at Lomita as I said thank you and goodbye? What if love was standing with me on the bank of the Truckee River, with me in the trees on Orcas Island, with me on the plane from the West Coast to the East Coast as we began the task of relocating and rebuilding?

And, what if love was lacing up her shoes every time I had to take Rosie out at the Lofts, walking right beside me, stride for stride? What if it was love that got me up and out and even, yes, bending down and picking up? What if love was right there every time I had to get in bed, taking slow breaths next to me?

What if love was there when I burrowed down into the leaves behind the new house, totally surrendered in corpse pose, asking for order in the midst of so much chaos? What if it was love that kept telling me to look, and then look again? What if love wanted me to see something I would have never seen had I not been laid entirely bare.

What if love was sitting in the rows of chairs, maybe even in every seat, in the backyard of the Hamiltons' home on the day of Ken's service?

What if love was in the thousands of acts of kindness that resuscitated me? Tina breaking into my house and setting my table with dinner and roses cut from her garden so that when we dragged in from baseball practice, it was all waiting for us. Jamie flying to me in California and Virginia and Virginia again. Kate sending the owl ornament to remind me that I'm wise. Ashley getting me to the gym. Laura and all that unsweet tea. Tatum texting prayers. Erica messaging memes. It goes on and on.

What if love was there in all the in-betweens, in the wildernesses of not knowing and not seeing, moving through it with me when I could, stopping when I couldn't?

Love spreads out her wings over us in the darkness, hovering, waiting. She shields and protects us as we are becoming what we were always intended to be. I picture my Warrior Sisters encircled around me. They are facing outward, soul sentries. They are armed, armored, glorious. Wildlings. Love does this.

Love calls us into the darkness, creates an impenetrable membrane around us while we go deep within, and brings to us the resources we need to continue. Love taps us on the shoulder and tells us it's time. Love reaches out a hand and invites us forward. Love does all that—infinite in its capacity and creativity.

We have an opportunity to emerge from the darkness more whole than when we went in. It all feels like loss and reduction. But at the bottom of the rubble, you will find a part of you that nothing can kill. Love leads us to her.

Dear Leeana,

Even in the midst of great loss, you have found your way back to yourself. You have become even more you. This has been spectacular to witness.

All my love,
Love

I recently had pictures taken of me, and I've had a number of people tell me that something strong was in my eyes. "You look so calm; I see a deep peace" and "The grounded confidence in your eyes is incredible" and "That photo is so tender and so fierce all at the same time."

These are different words than "You look beautiful," which are kind and generous words too. These say to me, "I see something in you that is noticeable and significant." Love took me on a terribly tumultuous journey. What the journey of love teaches us is that the treasure was in our front yard all along. We may have had to go looking for it Anywhere Else and in Everyone Else, but it's here. *Right here*. And it has been all along.

What if the love letter is specifically addressed to the YOU who got lost along the way? To remind you that love is bigger than anything that can be taken from you?

Go back and read all the words from the voice. Read them with the knowledge that they are coming from the Voice of Love:

Your person is you.

You already have everything you need to walk through this.

It's not all up to you.

Look again.

I will not let the storm consume you.

Peace. Be still.

Just because it's over doesn't mean it's gone.

Radical acceptance.

What brought you here will take you forward.

I hope love holds you hostage sometimes, wraps her arms around you, and refuses to let you go. I hope love whispers in your ear that your life and your story matter and that you are never, not for even one second, ever forgotten. I hope love holds your hand, a constant companion on whatever road you must walk. And I hope love helps you bear the weight of having a wide-open human heart in the midst of this wild and wondrous world.

I hope.

And I hope you do too.

HOLDING HOPE

God, what do you want to say
in your love letter to me?

a benediction

And Isaiah's word:

> There's the root of our ancestor Jesse,
> breaking through the earth and
> growing tree tall,
> Tall enough for everyone everywhere to
> see and take hope!

Oh! May the God of *green hope* fill you up with joy, fill you up with peace, so that your believing lives, filled with the life-giving energy of the Holy Spirit, will brim over with hope!

Romans 15:12–13

epilogue

YOUR TURN

HOPE _____ **ANYWAY: What Belongs in the Blank?**

I've shared twenty-seven different objects that I realized were worthy of my hope—even though making an investment in these twenty-seven was hard, counterintuitive, and unclear. I want to invite you, as I hope I have done throughout the book, to consider your own story one last time. What do you need to put your own hope in . . . anyway?

Maybe you want to borrow one of my phrases. Or maybe your reading and reflection have sparked something very specific to you. What belongs in the blank above? You could think of three possible categories:

Hope in God
Hope in Others
Hope in Yourself

Is there one of those categories that needs a reinvestment of your unrequited/scorned/spurned hope? Are you nursing a hope hangover, but you are being nudged to try again, to hope again?

This is a simple exercise, but it will also be telling. If there's one thing that needs your hope anyway, what is it?

surrendering practices

IGNATIAN INDIFFERENCE

Ignatian spirituality is a great thing to look into if you haven't already, as St. Ignatius offers us this beautiful concept and practice of "holy indifference," which we might also define as healthy detachment.

Our model for this holy indifference is Christ in the garden of Gethsemane: "Not my will but yours be done." We are not indifferent to God, to our own pain, to the situation. We are not saying "I don't care." We are asking God to give us the grace to be detached from the outcome. *Not my will but yours.*

Can I begin to relinquish the outcome? This happens through prayer. I sit and ask God to give me the grace to detach from my big plan.

Pray this as a breath prayer:

Not my will (on the inhale)
But yours be done (on the exhale)

As you exhale, imagine letting go of the thing or person or problem or behavior you are so deeply attached to.

SERENITY PRAYER AS A PRAYER OF SURRENDER

God, grant me the serenity
to accept the things I cannot change,
the courage to change the things I can,
and the wisdom to know the difference. Amen.

Pray through the above prayer every morning (twenty times a day if needed). Use it as a journaling prompt: God, what can I NOT change in the situation I'm facing? What CAN I change? Then write out what you hear from God and what comes up in your own spirit.

PAST, PRESENT, FUTURE

Are you struggling to surrender something from your past?

Are you struggling to surrender something that is happening in your present?

Are you struggling to surrender something that you are expecting of the future?

Use the above past, present, future questions as a journaling prompt. This will help you get clearer on what you might be holding on to.

WU WEI (PRONOUNCED "WOO WAY")

Wu wei is an important concept in Taoism. It is a Chinese word that is literally translated "non-doing." It means natural action, or in other words, action that does not involve struggle or excessive effort. "Wu wei is the cultivation of a mental state in which our actions are quite effortlessly in alignment with the flow of life."[1] Effortless action.

I often think of a willow tree. The wind blows through it and the branches flow and move. They are not rigid. Surrender is me being the willow tree, letting things come to me, move through, and pass on. I am not rigid and striving. I am the willow tree.

I find myself trying to make things happen or trying to figure things out. This is the opposite of Wu wei. When I want to force things in my own direction, I honestly picture the willow tree and I stop. I stop moving, trying, figuring. I decide to treat whatever it is as though it is not an urgent matter.

This has been a very helpful concept to me. Be the willow tree.

I SURRENDER MY DESIRE

Let's say you need to make a difficult phone call in order to create boundaries in a relationship. What are your desires around this specific conversation?

For things to go well? For you to be understood? For no one to be mad at you? For you to get the thing you want? For you to win? For you to come out looking good? For something or someone to change significantly?

Surrender everything you want to happen before you even begin the conversation:

God, I surrender my desire for this to go well.

God, I surrender my desire to be understood.

God, I surrender my desire to be validated.

God, I surrender . . .

We are all holding more desires and expectations than we will often admit. Take time to name how you want things to go, how you want to be perceived, what outcomes you are attached to. Surrender each and every one.

SPIRITUAL DIRECTION/THERAPY

Sometimes we are holding on so tightly to something and we are actually TOO terrified to let it go. We just can't. This is a good time to engage with a spiritual director or therapist. Perhaps there is trauma embedded in our bodies and we need help releasing that trauma. Perhaps some of our beliefs about God and his trustworthiness are wrapped up in our inability to let go.

These are important parts of our journey and process and cannot be overridden. We have to honor them, and we usually need the support of an empathetic other to help us untangle what's actually going on. Do you know how to find a trained spiritual director or counselor? If not, please reach out to me so I can help you get the support you need. My email address is leeana@leeanatankersley.com.

hope library

Acedia and Me, Kathleen Norris

All Along You Were Blooming, Morgan Harper Nichols

Almost Everything, Anne Lamott

The Anatomy of Hope, Jerome Groopman

Be the Bridge, Latasha Morrison

Bittersweet, Shauna Niequist

The Boy, the Mole, the Fox and the Horse, Charlie Mackesy

Breathing Under Water, Richard Rohr

Celebrations, Maya Angelou

Devotions, Mary Oliver

The Gifts of Imperfection, Brené Brown

A Grief Observed, C. S. Lewis

Healing the Shame That Binds You, John Bradshaw

Hope and Suffering, Desmond Tutu

Hope Heals, Katherine and Jay Wolf

Hope Rising, Casey Gwinn and Chan Hellman

The Hungering Dark, Frederick Buechner

I Know Why the Caged Bird Sings, Maya Angelou

The Inner Voice of Love, Henri J. M. Nouwen

Know My Name, Chanel Miller

Learning to Walk in the Dark, Barbara Brown Taylor

Love Is the Way, Bishop Michael Curry

The Next Right Thing, Emily P. Freeman

Option B, Sheryl Sandberg

A Severe Mercy, Sheldon Vanauken

There I Am, Ruthie Lindsey

Today, daily meditations from Emotions Anonymous

Traveling Mercies, Anne Lamott

Twilight Comes Twice, Ralph Fletcher

When the Heart Waits, Sue Monk Kidd

Wintering, Katherine May

Women, Food, and God, Geneen Roth

acknowledgments

So, just in case
I can't find
the perfect place—
"Thank you, thank you."

—Mary Oliver

WHILE THIS BOOK is the chronicle of my journey from "the news" to now, heartbreak to messy mending, it is also little more than a testimony of the gorgeous people in my life. An absolute embarrassment of riches. I hope that came through loud and clear.

But just in case, let me name some names.

Thank you to my agent, Angela Scheff of the Christopher Ferebee Agency, who gave me my first shot sixteen years ago and who continues to believe in me with the kind of unwavering fortitude that makes me wonder if she might be on to something.

Thank you to my editor, Andrea Doering, who gave me my second (and third, fourth, fifth, and sixth) shot seven years ago and who continues to champion my work as she makes it better than it could ever be without her.

I believe both of these women really *see* me, and I believe that matters greatly in my work and in my life. I have extraordinary respect for them both.

Thank you to the entire team at Revell who makes it their mission to get a beautifully crafted book in as many hands as possible—every single time. They are Eileen Hanson, Wendy Wetzel, Patti Brinks, Kristin Adkinson, William Overbeeke, their teams, and more.

Thank you to Elyse Miller and Elaine Hamilton for always reading early drafts with care and clarity.

Thank you to all of you who have read my work throughout the years and who have collectively nudged me to keep going.

Thank you to the MOPS International community for your support.

Thank you to my fiercely loyal, fiercely brilliant, and fiercely brave Warrior Sisters. These women have encircled me with the greatest care and the greatest courage: Ashley, Kara, Tatum, Jamie, Corrie, Tina, Linsey, Elaine, Debbie, Kate, Joanna, Wanida, Erica.

Thank you to the Miller, Hatfield, and Tankersley families. These last few years have not been an easy passage, and yet love has shown up in and through it all. I am incredibly grateful to be surrounded by such faithful family.

And thank you to my greatest gifts: Luke, Lane, and Elle. You three are the making of me.

Chapter 1 Hope in the Darkness Anyway

1. Barbara Brown Taylor, *Learning to Walk in the Dark* (New York: Harper-One, 2015), 129.
2. Elizabeth Gilbert (@elizabeth_gilbert_writer), Instagram post, October 21, 2020, https://www.instagram.com/p/CGm99hdhUuQ/.
3. Jeremiah 29:11.
4. Sue Monk Kidd, *The Book of Longing* (New York: Viking, 2020), 13.

Chapter 3 Hope in Your Self Anyway

1. Mary Karr, "Astonished by the Human Comedy," interview by Krista Tippett, *On Being* (podcast), orig. air date October 13, 2016, updated January 25, 2018, https://onbeing.org/programs/mary-karr-astonished-by-the-human-comedy-jan2018/.

Chapter 4 Hope in Grief Anyway

1. Emily Nagoski and Amelia Nagoski, *Burnout* (New York: Ballantine, 2020), xii.
2. Emily Dickinson, "After Great Pain a Formal Feeling Comes" (372), Poetry Foundation, https://www.poetryfoundation.org/poems/47651/after-great-pain-a-formal-feeling-comes-372. If you're a poetry kind of person, I encourage you to read Dickinson's poem, as it holds words you might need articulated.
3. See Luke 22:42.
4. Elisabeth Kübler-Ross and David Kessler, *On Grief and Grieving* (New York: Scriber, 2005).
5. David Kessler, *Finding Meaning* (New York: Scribner, 2020), 15 (emphasis added).

Chapter 6 Hope in Rebuilding Anyway

1. *Online Etymology Dictionary*, s.v. "regret," accessed November 14, 2020, https://www.etymonline.com/word/regret#etymonline_v_10335.

Chapter 7 Hope in What Saves You Anyway

1. Matthew 11:29.
2. Holly W. Whitcomb, *Seven Spiritual Gifts of Waiting* (Minneapolis: Augsburg Books, 2005), 24.
3. "Every step an arrival" comes from Denise Levertov's poem "Overland to the Islands," *Selected Poems* (New York: New Directions, 2002), 7.

Chapter 8 Hope in Mystery Anyway

1. Frederick Buechner, *The Hungering Dark* (New York: HarperOne, 1985), 116.

Chapter 9 Hope in Surrender Anyway

1. Genesis 1:1–2.
2. Desmond Tutu, *God Has a Dream* (New York: Doubleday, 2005), viii.

Chapter 10 Hope in Disappointment Anyway

1. Luke 24:19–21 NLT.
2. Buechner, *The Hungering Dark*, 121.

Chapter 11 Hope in Small Wonders Anyway

1. Psalm 13; Habakkuk 1:2.
2. Mary Oliver, "Don't Hesitate," in *Swan: Poems and Prose Poems* (Boston: Beacon Press, 2010), 42.

Chapter 12 Hope in Reality Anyway

1. Jerome Groopman, *The Anatomy of Hope* (New York: Random House, 2005), xvi.
2. Groopman, *The Anatomy of Hope*, xiv.

Chapter 13 Hope in Loss Anyway

1. Mary Oliver, "The Summer Day," *Devotions* (New York: Penguin, 2020), 316.
2. Anne Lamott, *Almost Everything* (New York: Riverhead, 2018), 183.
3. *Online Etymology Dictionary*, s.v. "apathy," accessed November 2, 2020, https://www.etymonline.com/word/apathy#etymonline_v_15451.
4. Buechner, *The Hungering Dark*, 121.
5. Hesiod, *The Works and Days*, trans. Richmond Lattimore (Ann Arbor: University of Michigan Press, 1991), 29.

Chapter 14 Hope in Holding On Anyway

1. Anne Lamott, *Bird by Bird* (New York: Anchor Books, 1994), 165.
2. Ecclesiastes 4:12 NLT.

Chapter 15 Hope in Your Truth Anyway

1. Gaslighting is "the act of undermining another person's reality by denying facts, the environment around them, or their feelings. Targets of gaslighting are manipulated into turning against their cognition, their emotions, and who they fundamentally are as people": Robin Stearn, "I've Counseled Hundreds of Victims of Gaslighting. Here's How to Spot If You're Being Gaslighted," Vox, updated January 3, 2019, 10:22 a.m. EST, https://www.vox.com/first-person/2018/12/19/18140830/gaslighting-relationships-politics-explained.

Chapter 16 Hope in Possibility Anyway

1. Elizabeth Gilbert, *Eat Pray Love* (New York: Riverhead Books, 2016), 94.

Chapter 17 Hope in Vulnerability Anyway

1. Luke 24:38–40 NLT.
2. David Whyte, "A Lyrical Bridge between Past, Present and Future," TED video, April 2017, https://www.ted.com/talks/david_whyte_a_lyrical_bridge_between_past_present_and_future?language=en (emphasis added).
3. You can hear David Whyte talk about these ideas on his TED Talk, "A Lyrical Bridge between Past, Present and Future."

Chapter 18 Hope in Healing the World Anyway

1. Lady Gaga, "Lady Gaga: Heal Through Kindness," interview by Oprah Winfrey, *Oprah's SuperSoul Conversations* (podcast), November 6, 2019, https://omny.fm/shows/oprah-s-supersoul-conversations/lady-gaga-heal-through-kindness.
2. Pádraig Ó Tuama, *In the Shelter* (London: Hodder & Stoughton, 2015), 86.
3. In 2014, poet Pádraig Ó Tuama was named the new leader of Corrymeela, Northern Ireland's oldest peace and reconciliation organization, founded in 1965 by Ray Davey, along with John Morrow and Alex Watson (learn more at www.corrymeela.org):

> For nearly 50 years the Corrymeela Community has promoted peace building and reconciliation from a Christian faith perspective. Current divisions within society reinforce the importance of that work. Members of the Community are delighted that Pádraig has accepted our invitation to be our new Leader. Pádraig has the skills and experience to build on the work of previous Leaders as we seek to fulfill our vision of embracing difference, healing division and enabling reconciliation.

John Hunter, Chairman of the Corrymeela Council, "Corrymeela Appoints Pádraig Ó Tuama as Community Leader," November 1, 2014, https://www.corrymeela.org/news/4/corrymeela-appoints-padraig-tuama-as.
4. Saint Augustine, "Augustin of Hippo Quotes," Goodreads, accessed November 14, 2020, https://www.goodreads.com/quotes/107417-hope-has-two-beautiful-daughters-their-names-are-anger-and.
5. See Ecclesiastes 3:11.

6. Jericho Brown, "The KR Conversation: Jericho Brown," *Kenyon Review*, accessed November 14, 2020, https://kenyonreview.org/conversation/jericho -brown/.

7. See the entire conversation in my book *Brazen* (Grand Rapids: Revell, 2016), 112–13.

Chapter 19 Hope in Crossing Over Anyway

1. You can order your own retreat box from Linsey at www.linseywildey .com. Run, don't walk. I'm serious.

2. This is a paraphrase of reflections that originally appeared in "With Jesus in the Storm: Rembrandt's Meditation," Soul Shepherding, https://www .soulshepherding.org/with-jesus-in-the-storm-on-the-sea-of-galilee-a-medi tation-on-rembrandts-painting/; and Juliet Benner, *Contemplative Vision* (Downers Grove, IL: InterVarsity, 2011), chap. 6.

Chapter 21 Hope in the Wilderness Anyway

1. Naomi Shihab Nye, "Kindness," *Everything Comes Next* (New York: Greenwillow Books, 2020), 222.

2. See Lamentations 3:22. Because of God's great love for us, we are not consumed.

3. Jeremiah 31:2–4 (emphasis added).

Chapter 23 Hope in What Brought You Here Anyway

1. Henri Nouwen, *The Inner Voice of Love* (New York: Doubleday, 1996), 21.

Chapter 24 Hope in Your Roots Anyway

1. Visit www.soulcarehouse.com/orcas for upcoming offerings.

2. For more on this, see Hannah Fries, *Forest Bathing Retreat* (North Adams, MA: Storey, 2018).

3. Phantom Forest, "How Many Trees Are Needed to Produce Enough Oxy- gen for One Person?," *Phantom Forest* (blog), September 26, 2016, http://blog .phantomforest.com/2016/09/how-many-trees-are-needed-to-produce-enough -oxygen-for-one-person/.

4. Diane Toomey, "Exploring How and Why Trees 'Talk' to Each Other," *E360*, Yale School of the Environment, September 1, 2016, https://e360.yale .edu/features/exploring_how_and_why_trees_talk_to_each_other.

Chapter 25 Hope in What Is Next Anyway

1. Anne Lamott, *Hallelujah Anyway* (New York: Riverhead Books, 2017), 37.

Chapter 27 Hope in Love Anyway

1. Barbara Kingsolver, "How to Survive This" in *How to Fly* (New York: HarperCollins, 2020), 9.

2. Read Katherine May's book *Wintering* (New York: Riverhead Books, 2020) to learn more about how to honor and inhabit the winter seasons of our lives.

Surrenduring Practices

1. Angélique Anjali Liao, "Wu Wei: Lau Tzu's Wisdom," Thrive Global, April 13, 2017, https://thriveglobal.com/stories/wu-wei-lao-tzu-s-wisdom/.

Leeana Tankersley is the author of six books, including *Breathing Room, Brazen, Begin Again*, and *Always We Begin Again*, and holds English degrees from Liberty University and West Virginia University. Leeana's writing has been featured on the *Huffington Post*, cnn.com, incourage.me, and aholyexperience.com. She is a regular contributor to MOPS International as both a writer and a speaker. Originally from Southern California, Leeana and her three kids now live in Central Virginia. Learn more at www.leeanatankersley.com.

CONNECT WITH

LEEANA TANKERSLEY

at LeeanaTankersley.com

- tankersleyleeana
- lmtankersley
- leeanatankersley

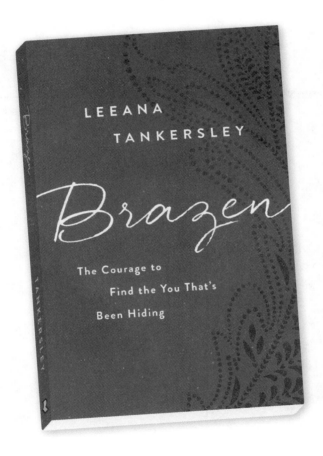

LET'S TALK ABOUT BOOKS

- Share or mention the book on your social media platforms. Use the hashtag **#HopeAnywayBook**.

- Write a book review on your blog or on a retailer site.

- Pick up a copy for friends, family, or anyone who you think would enjoy and be challenged by its message!

- Share this message on Twitter, Facebook, or Instagram: **I loved #HopeAnywayBook by @leeanatankersley //** **@RevellBooks**

- Recommend this book for your church, workplace, book club, or small group.

- Follow Revell on social media and tell us what you like.

 RevellBooks   RevellBooks   RevellBooks